# BAD CHILDHOOD— GOOD LIFE

# BAD CHILDHOOD—
# GOOD LIFE

## How to Blossom and Thrive
## in Spite of
## an Unhappy Childhood

# Dr. Laura Schlessinger

HarperCollins*Publishers*

HarperCollins books may be purchased for educational, business, or sales pro-motional use. For information, please write: Special Markets Department, HarperCollins Publishers, 10 East 53rd Street, New York, NY 10022.

FIRST EDITION

Designed by Elliott Beard

Printed on acid-free paper

Library of Congress Cataloging-in-Publication Data

Schlessinger, Laura.
    Bad childhood—good life : how to blossom and thrive in spite of an unhappy childhood / by Laura Schlessinger.—1st ed.
        p.   cm.
    ISBN-10: 0-06-057786-X
    ISBN-13: 978-0-06-057786-5
    1. Success—Psychological aspects.  2. Self-actualization (Psychology)
3. Blame.  4. Self-defeating behavior.  5. Child development.  I. Title.

BF637.S8S3385   2006
158.1—dc22                                        2005050243

06  07  08  09  10   ❖/RRD   10 9 8 7 6 5 4 3 2 1

**To all of you who must take this journey**

# Contents

# BAD CHILDHOOD—
# GOOD LIFE

# Introduction

For Lord's sake, here we go again. You had a miserable childhood. Your father was overbearing and your mother ignored you. What else is new? Chelsea, you have a great big chip on your shoulder, which is very unattractive. You stay away for years at a time. You never come home unless I beg you to and then when you do, all you can do is be disagreeable about the past. What is the point? Don't you think that everyone looks back on their childhood with a certain amount of bitterness and regret about something? It doesn't have to ruin your life, darling. You're a big girl now. Aren't you tired of it all? Bore, bore, bore. Life marches on, Chelsea, I suggest you get on with it.

**—Ethel (Katharine Hepburn) speaking to her
adult daughter, Chelsea (Jane Fonda),
in the movie version of *On Golden Pond***

*"Too many people blame their disappointments with their lives on their parents and the childhood they had. Please, that was ages ago. Let it go and move on,"* writes one of my listeners.

Sounds obvious. So why isn't it that simple? In January 2005, an eBay vendor was selling "Instant Happy Childhood Memories Breathspray." The description: "Instant Happy Childhood Memories Breathspray in Wintergreen Flavor will be a sure hit with its recipient. For the loved (or not so loved) one in your life who moans and complains about childhood and why his or her failings in life are mom's fault, dad's fault, your fault, or the dog's fault, this breath spray will help give them a new perspective on life." The back of the package reads: "Enjoy a sense of innocence, security and absolute well-being as you instantly remember fine family vacations, backyard playtime, and loving day-to-day activities at home with both a Mom and a Dad."

While this product was promoted as a "gag gift," I wonder how many people ordered it for themselves, or someone else, anyway . . . hoping.

While there has been a whole cottage industry dedicated to those who believe and identify themselves as injured or handicapped by their childhoods—commonly known as *victim, survivor, adult child of,* or those with *low self-esteem,* or from a *dysfunctional family*—I believe that many people don't even realize that their childhood history *has* impacted their adult thought and behavioral patterns in unproductive ways. They don't realize that some of their less pleasant or destructive adult emotional reactions are reflexive responses forged by their unfortunate childhood challenges. They don't realize that much of their adult life has been dedicated to repeating ugly childhood dynamics in an attempt to repair deep childhood hurts and longings. They're reduced to believing that neither they nor life matters much anyway, not understanding that they have the power and the choice to make a good life.

One of the most significant reasons why many people, especially those who identify themselves as victims of something or someone in their childhood, find it difficult to figure out a solution for an immediate dilemma is that they don't appreciate the specific effect of their early lives on their current style of thinking and feeling. For example, when callers tell me of a problem they often begin by saying, "I don't know why, but . . . ," which is an immediate tip-off that they are operating on two planes simultaneously: the past and the present. The emotional pull of the past, while often seemingly invisible to the person feeling confused and conflicted, is more powerful than the logic of the moment.

A quick and powerful example of this phenomenon is demonstrated in the following call I took from a young man, Chris, who was struggling with whether or not to "risk" having children.

CHRIS: I'm twenty-five years old and in May I will be successfully married for eight years. I don't have any kids at present and my wife and I are getting to the point of thinking about having children. My concern is, for some reason or another, and I don't know why—there is no history of it in my family—but in the back of my head I get real nervous and paranoid about my wife getting pregnant and giving birth to children with the risk of possible mental retardation or birth defects, to the point that it really puts me off about having children at all.

DR. LAURA: So, Chris, where did *you* learn you had to be perfect?

CHRIS: . . . (long silence) . . . Well, I, I haven't learned I have to be perfect.

DR. LAURA: Yeah, you have. So where did you learn it?

CHRIS: . . . (another long silence) . . . Well, I feel that . . .

DR. LAURA: I want you to answer my question. I didn't ask you about your feelings. Where did you learn you have to be perfect?

CHRIS: Maybe just from growing up. I have to do everything correctly, or perfect, as you call it. I try to do everything to the best of my ability in everything I do.

DR. LAURA: There is a difference between having a sense of responsibility to put your best effort out, and having no value unless you're perfect. You are more in the latter category. And because of that, you're afraid that through your children something imperfect will happen, and then you will no longer be worthy anymore.

CHRIS: . . . (quietly) . . . Yes.

DR. LAURA: And frankly, my dear, if your children had special needs and you rose to the occasion, it would prove you most worthy. Think about that.

Here is Chris, a twenty-five-year-old man, married for eight years, unaware that the demands on him from his childhood to be perfect were contaminating his adult decisions about making a family.

If he were only living in the present, Chris's logic would determine that medically there was little elevated risk of his children having a problem considering the age, health, and family history of Chris and his wife. Also, tragic results are not typically foremost on a young adult's mind when he or she thinks of having a family; time crunches, no sleep, and finances are. But because of the pull for perfection from his childhood, Chris's emotions are churning, "for reasons he doesn't understand," over the reality that creating perfectly healthy and competent children is largely out of his control, putting him at risk of failing in his parents' eyes. And this would be true even if both his parents were deceased! That feeling of failure, being inadequate and disappointing to a parent, outlives even that parent.

While people may be quite aware of their early life challenges, they still may be seriously unaware of how *their choices* in people, environments, decisions, behaviors, and attitudes are connected to those experiences, and how those choices are the major factor in their current predicaments and unhappiness.

An unfortunate example of this lack of awareness, and almost lemminglike drive to go over a cliff, is demonstrated by Janeen's call to my radio program. Janeen is a woman in her late twenties, married, with two very young children. She called, crying, to tell me that she just didn't know what to do about the fact that her brother killed himself in her home where her children would be first to find him. I asked her if she had any notion as to his motive. She said she didn't really know, other than that she had brought him into her home to live, but things were going badly, and just the night before his suicide, she had asked him to leave.

I pointed out the hostility of his act, and asked her if he had always "been a difficult problem," and she answered affirmatively. When I asked her why she would put her husband and children through those problems by bringing a seriously troubled brother into their home, she literally had no answer. No matter how much I pushed and prodded, she had no answer. We struggled together for several minutes when I finally suggested that she talk to her husband, who had not been happy about bringing her brother into their home, to try to have some understanding about what drove her to attempt to rescue and fix him.

We made an agreement that we would talk the next day.

Janeen called right on time and sounded like a different woman. I repeated the question, "Why would you bring these problems with your brother into your home?" She had the answer, and said she had to be really honest with herself, instead of soaking in denial.

"My brother blamed me for everything. And I decided to own it. I was filled with guilt and I tried to fix the problem," she admitted.

"Well, Janeen, your rational mind should know that you couldn't possibly be responsible for all your brother's problems and pains, right?"

"Actually, I guess I thought I was responsible. I helped raise him. My mother was divorced and always at work. I was the one to raise him."

"So you think because he was messing up his life that this was your fault?"

"Yes."

"Janeen, if your brother was 'messed up,' let's look at the larger truth. Your father was absent and your mother was busy. He didn't have a parent. You did the best you could, but you were a kid. Kids can't really raise kids. Why do you think he didn't commit suicide at your mother's house? I guess he was protecting what little he had with her or he was in massive denial. I think you've been in denial also—taking all this responsibility on yourself. No wonder you brought him into your home; it's how you tried to fix the 'bad mothering' you think you did. But that was the past you both shared. You both suffered from the loss of Mommy and Daddy. You denied your childhood angst by burying yourself in your brother and his issues. Your brother denied his childhood angst by blaming you—which fed into your denial . . . and so it went, around and around."

"I agree one hundred percent."

Until I had challenged her decision to bring her brother into her home during our first conversation, she was like a "mis"guided missile—blindly trying to make up to her brother what she identified as her "bad mothering" of him, when in fact neither one of them wanted to confront the fact that they both were virtually abandoned by both parents. However, Janeen had made better life choices, was educated, married, and a mother. Her brother, jealous, resented all she had, and wanted to hurt his "surrogate mother." Sick. Sad.

After our second talk, Janeen felt freer of that consuming, irrational guilt that made her put her own family second to an attempt to resolve the emotional devastation of her birth family.

Actually, I have often been surprised when, after I draw a connection between their early family dynamics and their current attitudes or decisions, a caller—ostensibly fully aware of his or her own history, and even after years and years of psychotherapy—will say, "Ah-ha! I never thought of that. I never saw it that way."

It is one thing to know that since you were terrorized by a nasty dog when you were eight years old you now fear dogs; it is another thing altogether to realize that since you witnessed your father terrorizing your meek mother you now take the role of your father simply to avoid being a victim like your mother—as though predator or prey were the only viable alternatives. The former situation shows good sense in cautionary behavior around growling dogs. The latter situation shows that as an adult, you are viewing all human interactions only through the myopic lens of your early childhood family life.

Early coping and defensive strategies often become habits, and habits are behaviors that are reflexive, repetitive, and without much conscious thought. People generally do not recognize that their current behaviors were perhaps suited to their childhood circumstances, but not their immediate situations or relationships. That's why these behaviors and ways of thinking and interpreting events and others' intentions are usually "off," not constructive, and annoying to others.

Many of my callers give evidence of this dynamic. A typical example is the reasonable reaction of not trusting a parent who made promises that were never realized. Coping mechanisms range from being clingy to finding reasons to keep a safe emotional distance. When in adulthood this once-betrayed individual is constantly testing, confronting, and/or accusing everyone who tries to get close as though they were untrustworthy, without any evidence to support that claim, clearly this person is generalizing from the disappointing parent to all potential intimates—ultimately avoiding closeness for fear of hurt.

Then there are those who quite consciously choose to live with a scarlet "V" for victim on their chests. These folks are so scared of the risks involved in change that they hold onto suffering. That suffering also offers "secondary gains." Secondary gains are psychological and interpersonal "perks." These perks mostly revolve around protecting themselves by controlling others through demanding concessions because of their hurt or fears, or "discomforts."

With this victim identity in mind, Kenneth, one of my listeners, wrote to me in response to a call he heard in which a woman was holding onto her past so dearly that she was missing the beauty of the possibilities of each new day: "*Surely your skills as a therapist include familiarity with that 'warm bag of poop' so many of us carry around with us. Imagining a real bag of offal makes it clear that a rational person would simply discard or bury the bag. But we humans often insist on keeping that bag with us. From time to time we dip our hand into the bag and stir it up. Yes, it stinks and yes it is offensive, but it's OUR bag of poop and we're familiar with how it smells, how it feels, and we are comforted by that warm feeling of familiarity we often get from it. If we let it go, bury it, or dispose of it, what do we have left that defines us? I guess we'll have to create a new 'us' if we don't have that stinky bag of poop to define us."*

I want to make it clear that nobody enjoys being in emotional pain. They are not, as is often heard in the vernacular, "getting off on it." No way. It is all about fear and an inward self-focus that developed out of a need to protect oneself and survive one's childhood. Unfortunately, much of the popular therapeutic view and pop psych mentality has functioned to keep people in self-pitying, victim mode mentality, robbing them of optimism, confidence, hope, growth, and change.

Gail, one of my listeners, wrote about falling into this trap: *"In my case, it had never occurred to me to think of myself as a casualty of my bad childhood until I was acknowledged as such by another person. This gave me permission to revel in my victimhood and discuss it seemingly evermore with all who would commiserate. It was never hard to find willing participants, as there were many who were eager to find fault with their parents.*

*"The turning point for me came when I listened to an answering machine tape of my sister and myself discussing our parents and how they were to blame for our unhappy lives. I was embarrassed as I heard myself holding them responsible for ALL of my misery, and I hadn't been under their roof in over ten years!*

*"At this point I, figuratively speaking, 'pulled a Moses.' I isolated myself for several months from anyone who would allow me to perpetuate that wrong thinking. I surrendered myself to the acceptance of my own responsibility for the conditions of my present life. Ultimately, I discovered that there is power in surrender—as my life improved, so did my relationship with my parents."*

A "poor me" mentality is understandable. It is terrible to

have been hurt, tortured, molested, abandoned, ignored, threatened, used, degraded, neglected, browbeaten, harassed, triangulated into parental or familial sick behaviors, or exposed to other demoralizing or dehumanizing behaviors. For anyone to minimize that truth is somewhere between ignorant and insensitive.

Many such "victims" find their own lifelong victimhood mode a frustrating, draining, unsuccessful, and unhappy way to live. Gerri, a listener, was sexually abused by a stepbrother at the age of ten after being adopted at birth by parents who divorced when she was four. *"I grew up with a total victim mentality. All the turmoil carved a pathway of 'poor me' in my brain that was very difficult to climb out of. Anything I did that was destructive or just plain wrong, I blamed on my 'dysfunctional childhood.' I am twenty-seven now and am turning into a 'victor.' I have come to realize (through my faith and understanding in God) that no matter where we come from or what circumstances have come into our lives, we are responsible for how we react to them. The biblical story of Joseph is a prime example.\**

*"From time to time, I do feel a little sorry for myself when I wish my relationships with my adoptive mother and father were closer and more open . . . but I realize that to go over the past is to never move forward.*

*"My advice to others is to simply decide where you want to go and start moving. Do you want a happy life filled with love and stability? Then you have to be the one to start moving in that direction.*

---

\*The jealous siblings of Joseph, Jacob's favorite son, expedite his demise, only to have a surprise reunion years later when famine causes them to come to Egypt for help. Through an amazing series of events, Joseph has become the right hand of the Pharaoh and is gracious to his brothers.

*It's all about your right to choice. You can choose to live in the past and feel about what may have happened to you or what you lost, or you can acknowledge your past and move on. You can never reach your future if you won't remove yourself from your past."*

"From time to time, I do feel a little sorry for myself . . . ," Gerri admits. This is a very important point. The truth about growth and change in attitudes and behaviors is twofold. First, changing behaviors and attitudes is a more effective way of influencing feelings than waiting for feelings (irrational, unpredictable, uncontrollable) to change before we make positive moves in our lives. Second, change and growth are not straight lines; one needs to learn to bear some scars and pains forever, as they ebb and flow in our hearts and brains with the natural tides of life's experiences and challenges. There is no way to eradicate horrendous memories from a difficult childhood.

But as Teresa, another listener, wrote: *"It is too easy to wallow in self pity. What happened, happened. I decided to become better than the monster and win the battle. What happened to me in my childhood was not my fault. How I handle it is my responsibility."*

While Teresa's courageous sentiment is right on, truth be told, change is challenging, painful, difficult, and often most frustrating as you find yourself in old patterns of thought and action before you even realize it! This is confirmed by Ann, a listener who wrote: *"Difficult parents train us to self-deprecate, self-loathe. My parents ripped up their proverbial parent card, as you often say on your program, Dr. Laura, and I still have an internal mess to work at. Here I want to change and it is extremely difficult and time-consuming. As I see and feel it, the crazy-making of these difficult parents lives on and internalizes."*

Tina came to that realization also: *"At one time I thought, great, I'm healed, thank you God! I'm normal now . . . let's get on with life. Lo and behold, I enter another phase of life (i.e., marriage, having kids, etc. . . .) and I find I have to go through another phase of healing. At first I resented the fact that I keep having to revisit these painful issues, but I now realize that God wants me to go deeper and deeper into the healing as I go through my adult life."*

Even in a serious state of denial, you know you've been hurt and damaged in ways that cause you confusion, pain, fear, and even anger. While you may be clear on the big picture of the difficulties you experienced in childhood, the "fine details" may not be so obvious. And, my friends, life is in the details.

Those fine details have to do with:

- how specifically your early childhood pain is in control today of your responses to people
- willingness to take risks, openness to love and friendship
- trust in people
- compulsive actions and obsessive thoughts directed toward getting attention and love
- fixing everyone and everything to make up for the sense of powerlessness as a child
- constantly creating in your adulthood your early bad situations in order to magically fix yesterday, and so forth

What this all means is that now your life is compounded with the pain of "yesterday," mixed with the disappointments and frustrations of "today." Many try to survive each day using promiscuity, drugs, alcohol, work, and other compulsive behaviors to drown out the inner noise of hurt, anger, and despair. At some point, though, it has to become clear that these attempts to avoid pain paradoxically bring even more pain and problems.

Those who have successfully overcome victimhood force

themselves in directions they know are healthy, in spite of tremendous doubts and fears that pull them back. Julie, another listener, describes this as tapping into "a strong will," without which a *"life is doomed to alcoholism or drug abuse. A strong will is required for a lifetime. I know that I don't dote on my childhood. I don't look back very often or with any great depth. I don't think about all the 'what ifs.'*

"*When you come from a bad childhood, I think it makes you less sympathetic for anyone who uses it as a crutch for every poor decision they have made with their lives. I do think of myself as a compassionate person, but I always find myself asking the question, 'What is the difference between me and him (her)?' The difference is that I have a faint memory when I was about eight years old, after a particularly violent argument between my two very drunk parents, of making a somewhat conscious promise to myself that someday I would 'make' a good life for myself.*

"*I hung on to that promise. I made it happen—and I don't look back.*"

Most people who e-mailed and faxed me their reflections on *Bad Childhood—Good Life* after I mentioned on air that I was working on this book mentioned that pure grit became more potent when there was somebody there for them, someone who believed in them and could be trusted to be there.

For most people, it would seem that somebody was God. Amy wrote to me that verses from Psalm 27 became her song and theme: "If my father and my mother have forsaken me, the LORD will take me up." "I am filling my void with God," she wrote.

Why does a relationship with God help so many people? I believe the answer is manifold. First, people feel loved and therefore worthy and valuable. Second, religious values and commandments give them direction when they may not ever have been taught morals or about resisting temptations. Temptations, with their immediate gratification, are attractive to people with pain and rage. Third, a religious perspective is outward-focused, while victimhood is inward-focused.

Lori wrote about the benevolent influence of religious commitment in helping personal healing: *"Finding a higher purpose in life has really helped. I try to be of help whenever I can. I try to remember to be of service to God. Giving and caring for others is so much more rewarding than being in my own head. When I realized that what I hated was not so much this world—but what was in my mind—good growth and changes starting happening."*

I don't believe anyone does life well alone; I believe you lose your humanity by isolating yourself. This might mean you have to start with AA, psychotherapy, or a prayer group. It is up to you to reach out. The intent of *Bad Childhood— Good Life* is to help you accept the truth of the assault on your psyche, understand your unique coping style and how it impacts your daily thoughts and actions, and guide you into a life of more peace and happiness.

It is often very scary to be vulnerable, to trust, and to love when what you've learned about these behaviors as a child makes avoidance seem a reasonable and sane reaction. If you don't do this hard work, then your childhood was lost (not in your control), and now you've virtually decided to become your own abuser, robbing yourself of a peaceful, joyful, fulfilling, challenging, exciting life (in your control).

If you don't do this hard work, your decisions might lead you to directly or indirectly victimize a child. Carol wrote about this. *"His deep feelings regarding his life at home with a drunk father (like mine) will always be with him—and for that I am truly sorry I did not divorce much sooner. Please get out of a bad marriage, and do not let abuse be passed down to another generation.*

*"I live alone now because I have found I cannot bring my baggage into another relationship. My children do well, but the scars show in many of their relationships. I try to help with advice when I see things get out of hand and can only hope they all find peace and love in their lives."*

My heart goes out to all the Carols who are trying to play catch-up with the innocent victims of their own childhood struggles: their own children. When parents call and tell me of their children's misbehaviors, which are clearly a response to the chaos their foolish and psychologically blind choices have created, I tell them to apologize to their children for the mess they have made of their children's lives. I also tell them to point out to their children that his or her rebellious acting out is a self-destructive way to handle bitterness, frustrations, and disappointments—which are reasonable responses to unreasonable situations.

In other words, validate their perceptions and feelings about a bad childhood, but remind them that what they do about it will more definitively set the course for the rest of their lives; they get to aim for hell or heaven.

You should not be satisfied with being a victim, nor with being a survivor. You should aim to be, as Chandelle, a listener, suggested, *"a conquerer." "It was conquering my childhood,"* she wrote, *"not surviving it, which has made me the strong person that I am today."*

There is an extraordinary quality of spirit that leads one to aspire to conquering, rather than surviving. I hope to help you discover that spirit in yourself.

Remember, one day you're going to be but a footnote in the history of the world. What are you going to do between right now . . . and then?

# ONE

# To Be or Not to Be . . . a Victim

*Even flowers have to grow through dirt.*

—Nancy, a listener

Unfortunately, a lot of people are made to suffer as children: beatings, rapes, torture, abandonment, neglect, parental divorce and subsequent remarriage with new or stepchildren to compete with, alcoholic or drug-addicted parent(s), erratic and even dangerous consequences of parental mental illness, browbeatings, parental insensitivity, psychological and emotional assaults, parental affairs, constant family turmoil, molestations, familial violence, single parent by choice or irresponsibility, and so forth. They are definitely victims of self-centered, evil, ignorant, and/or weak adults; and, for me, weakness or ignorance do not excuse the resultant harm.

## In the Beginning . . .

More and more, the calls to my radio program are coming from children, children being victimized by their parents. I try, in the short time available to me in a live radio phone conversation, to do something to align that hurting child with something positive to hold onto. Samantha, for example, is a nine-year-old child who called wanting to know how to deal with a mother who won't take care of her and a father who is in and out of jail.

DR. LAURA: Where are you living?

SAMANTHA: I'm living with my grandma.

DR. LAURA: Your grandma? Is your grandpa there, too?

SAMANTHA: Uh-huh.

DR. LAURA: Are you a religious girl?

SAMANTHA: Yes.

DR. LAURA: This is what I suggest you do to deal with it. I suggest that every now and then you pray to God, and say, "God, thank you, thank you, thank you for giving me a grandma and grandpa to take care of me."

SAMANTHA: Okay.

DR. LAURA: Do you understand why I said that?

SAMANTHA: Sort of.

DR. LAURA: In our lives, we are going to have many disappointments. That goes for everybody, Samantha. Everybody. Some disappointments are bigger than others. Having two parents you can't count on is a huge disappointment. Huge. Huge. I understand you being hurt and disappointed and upset and angry and all kinds of stuff. Now, there are two kinds of people in this world. There are the people who have those big disappointments and they spend their lives being sad. And then there are the other people, who go, "It is sad that I have these disappointments, but I am sooo lucky because I have . . ." Samantha, which do you think are the happier people?

SAMANTHA: The people who are sad—but still happy.

DR. LAURA: Yup. That's going to be you, Samantha. That's
how you are going to deal with it. You are going to be sad
that you can't count on your mommy and daddy, but you
are going to be happy because there are people you *can*
count on. And you are going to make a happy life.

SAMANTHA: Okay. Bye. Thank you.

Getting calls like Samantha's, and there are too many, is
the worst and best of all worlds. I ache that these children are
hurting. I rejoice that they call me and that I can give them a
perspective that will hopefully detour them from a life of a
victimhood mentality.

Connor, an eleven-year-old boy, is "having a little dad
problem." It seems that his mom and dad have been divorced
for as long as he could remember (since he was four), and
every time he sees his dad and then has to leave, it causes him
so much pain.

CONNOR: I just can't bear to see him leave anymore. Even
if that means I can't even see him again.

DR. LAURA: Connor, do you like spaghetti?

CONNOR: What does that have to do with the topic? [Good
question, actually.]

DR. LAURA: Well, do you like spaghetti?

CONNOR: Yeah, why?

DR. LAURA: Do you like spaghetti and meatballs?

CONNOR: [getting impatient] Yeah.

DR. LAURA. I love spaghetti and meatballs. It's probably one
of my favorite meals. What you are telling me, Connor, is
that since I can only have two meatballs, and I can't have
the three that I want, that I might just as well not eat any
spaghetti and meatballs at all!

CONNOR: But I just can't take seeing him leave anymore.

DR. LAURA: It's the price you pay. And everything has a price attached to it, Connor. You want to see your dad? The price you have to pay is that it hurts when he goes. But the good part is that you get to see him. I pump iron. I can't say I love to do it, but I do it because it is the price to pay to be healthy and look good. I like having muscles! Everything has a price. For everything you really want, there's *something* you have to put up with.

CONNOR: Thank you, Dr. Laura

In speaking to Samantha and Connor, I had the opportunity to reframe a bad situation into a life lesson. Samantha learned about not ignoring the blessings (loving, caretaking grandparents) because of the curses (parental abandonment). Connor learned that life generally exacts a price (like painful goodbyes) for those things that are desired and meaningful (visitation with Dad).

Children need to learn at an early age that these lessons are universal experiences, not just their personal, unique, horrible cross to bear. It is easier for children to cope with difficult, even horrendous situations when they understand and accept that the advice they are getting is truths about life for all time and all people—not just an attempt to manipulate them out of justified hurt or angry feelings. While these are truths about a good life for all people, they are essential lessons for these victimized children.

As children get older, their ability to act out their hurt and anger with drugs, sex, truancy, and violence toward themselves or others becomes a serious concern. That is why it is so desperately important that these youngsters have someone they can turn to and count on. A mentor, family friend or relative, teacher, neighbor, clergy—someone needs to be there as that source of caring and hope. When that's not the case, there are others to fill in: pedophiles, gangsters, users, and so forth.

Todd, a fifteen-year-old boy, is at just that crossroads. He called me about his relationship with his mother. His father died when he was younger and his mother had divorced his stepfather four years earlier. After that divorce, she became exceedingly violent toward him—even going so far as to hit him with a baseball bat. He ran away a few times in despair and fear. His mother gave up her parental rights because "she couldn't put up with me anymore." He is living with her parents.

TODD: I try to make amends with her for whatever happened. But every time I try to talk to her she either yells at me or tells me I'm no good. She does the same thing to her parents, too.

DR. LAURA: Does that make you realize that her behavior isn't about you?

TODD: Yes, it does.

DR. LAURA: Okay, because you were saying that you have to make amends. The implication is that you thought you did something bad and you have to make it better. But the way you describe her behavior, it sounds like she's the problem, not you. Do you have clarity there?

TODD: Yes.

Todd's grandparents don't really say much about Todd's mother, their daughter. They just tell him that she is going through a tough time. It is clear that they are being somewhat protective of her, but at least they are still making it clear to Todd that the problem is her behavior and not his.

DR. LAURA: What is your question for me?
TODD: What can I do to make it better for her? I want just to be able to talk to her.

Keep in mind that at this point, Todd is an orphan; one parent is dead, a stepparent is gone, and his mother is venomously dangerous. It is natural for a child to want to get back a "mommy" if he can.

DR. LAURA: Nothing. Your job is going to be that you make sure you don't derail your life because of your pain about your mother. *That* is your job. That's the only place you have control. You can't fix her. You have to make sure you don't mess yourself up now. A lot of kids in your position do just that: get into drugs, crime, violence, sex—all sorts of things to display they anger and hurt, and to make themselves feel better at the moment. That's not a good plan! But it is all too typical. Have you started any of that yet?
TODD: No.
DR. LAURA: Good. Your job is not to try to change your mother. That's her job. Your job is not to mess up your life because you're angry and hurt. Do you think you can do that?
TODD: Yeah.
DR. LAURA: If you stay on the straight and narrow and healthy, when her brain gets straightened out, she'll have somebody wonderful to interact with. But if you mess up your life, it just messes things up more.
TODD: Okay, I hear what you're saying. I just needed to hear that from somebody I trust and respect.

I felt at the time that Todd was relieved that he was not responsible for his mother's decline or future rebound. Unfortunately, there are too many children who experience even worse assaults on their innocence, minds, and bodies who then go out into the world as aching hearts yearning for peace and happiness, but not having any clue as to how to attain it. Many of them turn into adults who flounder, fail, struggle, suffer, and often, as the cycle goes, indirectly or directly hurt their own children.

## And Then . . .

And then . . . many folks just stay stuck in their childhood ugliness—for decades, sometimes forever, angry, bitter, self-destructive, depressed, anxious, or just generally out of control and way off any positive track. In a way, these folks become career victims, always unhappy, unbelievably demanding of others, a big chip on the shoulder, an even bigger attitude of entitlement, and generally a propensity for spreading ill cheer. I'd watch family and friends sacrifice and bend over beyond backwards to cater to, support, sacrifice for, take care of, and give in to these people, all in the benevolent hope that they could lay on of hands and "heal," to minimally have peace in their own lives.

While I suppose it is possible to sometimes make the case that a person was so traumatized and at such a vulnerable time in their lives that it became impossible for them ever to be happy or functional, I don't buy it. I do buy that it is a lot harder for some, due to their particular personality traits or magnitude of childhood problems, than others to take back their opportunities and potential. When I was in private practice, I saw people I thought were so damaged that perhaps they could not possibly pull a positive life together. I would sit, week after week, in awe of their grit and spirit in making the better (always scary) choices to improve their lives. Then there were the others who seemed to have so much going for them, with minimal external restraints, who almost seemed determined to not progress past the first chapter of their lives.

The obvious question is, "What makes some people hold onto being a victim and others choose to improve their lives?" The answer is control. When you are a perpetual victim, the past is in control of your present. When you are a conqueror, the present is controlled by your choices, in spite of the pain and pull of your past.

Inspiring, isn't it? Yet it is so difficult for some people to make up their minds and follow through, to become conquerors. Why? There are at least nine reasons, all having to do with an emotional attachment to certain kinds of crutches. These emotional attachments become *bad habits*.

## 1. Identity

When the *very first* thing a caller to my radio program does to present or introduce themselves to me is to let me know that they:

- come from a *dysfunctional* family
- are a *survivor* of . . . some egregious parental behavior (alcoholism, drug abuse, violence, neglect, abandonment, divorce, annoying, destructive, unpredictable) or experience (molestation, having been picked on for some trait/behavior)
- are in *constant hurt*, demonstrated by immediately *crying or choking up* as a style of introductory communication
- have *low self-esteem* because of their childhood
- are "sensitive"

I then know up front that they do not perceive themselves as individuals *with* a past, but as individuals totally *defined by* the past.

Chelsea, a listener, wrote that, "*Continuing to be a victim is something that . . . people do in an attempt to find value in themselves. The sad part is that their idea of value is twisted to believe that being a part of something negative makes them important.*"

With all the workshops, seminars, tapes, books, groups, therapies, TV specials and programs, clubs, and internet chat rooms there are for those who have, or believe they have, experienced childhood hardship, it is natural that some people would gravitate toward them to feel a sense of comfort in belonging. Unfortunately, some people stay stuck in their destructive and negative thought processes and behaviors just because it is the price of admission to belonging to a group of "like" people. Staying stuck in this victim mode means "having company;" therefore, moving on becomes a threat of loneliness and emotional risk.

It is true that many of those venues have helped people feel safe to admit to painful truths of their childhood, have supported those with the grit and commitment to move forward with their lives, and have given many folks resources for help. However, it is also true that there is a sublime status given to those who have suffered, as well as a neverending wellspring of compassion, understanding, affection—and attention—that is hard to give up.

A victim identity becomes a bad habit.

## 2. Rewards

Indulging in the miserable demands attention and sympathy. Most folks have good hearts and want nothing more than to relieve another of their pain. Too many of these well-meaning folks sacrifice too much of their lives and energy to doing that in spite of evidence that it just isn't working. Yet they feel guilty to give it up. These relationships are painfully one-sided, because the "sufferer" is perpetually needy and therefore unavailable for reciprocation.

"I think that those who play the victim are rewarded for it. They choose to surround themselves with people who will put up with it and cater to them. It's hard to face the truth and change. I know I had a turning moment in my life when my husband, who was then my boyfriend, after listening to yet another rant about how terrible my father is and poor me, blah-blah-blah, looked me in the eye and asked, 'For how long are you going to be mad at your father?' I started bawling and literally felt myself letting go of the anger and weight and blame. I could tell, from the look in his eye, that he would not put up with a lifetime of 'bad father stories' and 'pity me parties.' He wanted a healthy woman and I wanted a lifetime with him. So, I changed and the reward was great.

"My sister's husband, however, puts up with her whiny, I-am-your-baby-girl voice she puts on when she wants to manipulate him into doing something for her. My brother's choices of girlfriends are forever getting younger, less mature and secure, and expect less and less from him. That's what they choose.

"I chose differently," wrote an anonymous listener.

It is hard to face the truth and make changes in one's life. It takes hard work. And the fact is that many people surround themselves with people who allow them to be stuck. These people are afraid to tell their friend or partner the truth lest they hurt their feelings. Sadly, hurting feelings has risen in our society to the status of a high crime, and that's too bad, because temporary hurt feelings that lead to an awakening of positive possibilities are a small price to pay to literally save a life from wasted misery.

Rewards become a habit.

## 3. Routine

Let's face it, the familiar, even when it is unproductive or ugly, is "comfortable." Yes, even pain can be comfortable. At least you know what to expect and, you have developed ways of not being too overwhelmed by the unknown.

For example, there are those people who hold on too tightly to the notion that since their parents were unloving toward them, they must be unlovable. Hence, they either keep themselves isolated, or always manage to be in relationships with unloving and unlovable types. Although these relationships are hurtful and disappointing, they already know what to expect and how to handle it, and so they are too afraid to give them up. Instead, they talk about hope, how they probably deserve or how they must somehow have provoked their partner's bad behavior.

The thought of risking a relationship with a loving person who could possibly not love them after getting to know them is way too threatening than not having the love of a difficult person who can't love anyway.

One thirty-three-year-old woman called with her question, but when she started with the fact that she'd been dating this guy for thirteen years, on and off, I took it from there.

DR. LAURA: What is the point of dating someone for thirteen years? What happened to the notion that after two years some decision should be made about a marital commitment?

JENNIFER: Well, there have been problems. And I just started living with him . . .

DR. LAURA: Married people live together, unmarried people are shacking up because they don't want to be lonely but they don't want to be obligated—and obligation is one of the major aspects of love.

JENNIFER: Okay, shacking up. Then I found out that he's been having an affair for four years with another woman.

DR. LAURA: So, after thirteen tumultuous years, a shack-up without a commitment, and a four-year affair behind your back . . . what is your question?

JENNIFER: Should I confront him about the affair?

DR. LAURA: [at top of lungs] Why? What would be the point? You want him to say, "Oops, sorry, she really didn't mean anything to me for the four years I have been having sex with her, giving her gifts, and telling her 'I love you' behind your back—I really love you, honey"? That doesn't sound, forgive me, stupid?

JENNIFER: Well, I still have hope for this relationship.

DR. LAURA: No, it's not that you have hope for this relationship—it's that you're too scared of a real relationship. Think about this and we'll talk again when you're ready to look at it. The key here is a lack of outrage. Instead, you're ready to just go on with it. As sick as this is, it's clearly a place you, sadly, feel comfortable.

JENNIFER: It will probably have something to do with my childhood.

DR. LAURA: Probably. Hopefully you'll give this a lot of thought.

Familiar routines become a bad habit.

## 4. Revenge

When I was in private practice I worked with a large number of teens and young adults who seemed hellbent on being destructive. These were young people who otherwise indicated great potential personally and professionally. Yet they were willing to deep-six the positive possibilities for their futures for the sake of wreaking havoc. They would fail and have to come home. They would end up in psych wards or jail cells. They would put their families through hell, as parents and siblings tried to rescue, placate, support, threaten, or lecture them about illegal or risky or self-destructive behaviors with drugs, risky sex that will lead to illegitimate children or disease, unsafe driving, or misdemeanors and felonies.

What I would discover is that many of these young people were getting their revenge on a family life that hurt or disappointed them. They imagined that these horrific behaviors were the key to taking the power and control they didn't feel as children. They also had found an obvious outlet for all their anger and the self-doubt that resulted from their early family problems.

Some of it was more specific. If a particular parent, for example, viciously demeaned them about not excelling enough in academics or athletics, they would intentionally cause themselves to fail or get kicked out. If a particular parent was unbearably controlling about looks or dress, they would go the complete opposite, with body piercing and grunge clothes and becoming excessively fat or thin.

It was also startling to see how often they would get revenge on the nonabusive, "good" parent who didn't protect them by abusing and hurting that so-called "good" parent the way they as children had been abused by the "bad" parent.

They might also do the same toward siblings who were doing better in their own lives.

Revenge becomes a bad habit.

## 5. Dependency

Many adults who were starved for affection, attention, and approval as children often burden others with a feeling of responsibility for their happiness. They begrudge their family members', spouse's, and friends' activities, hobbies, accomplishments, friends, interests, growth, and happiness. They are like vampires, having to live on the life's blood of others, always demanding, never filled up, always sad, always needing more, never satisfied, never happy. Their friends and relatives have to hide their joys and successes so as not to "hurt" the "victim," and also to avoid the repercussions, which range from fits of depression, to bouts of anger and recrimination, to outbursts about their sad history, personal losses, bad luck, hurt feelings, and pain.

Dependency becomes a habit.

## 6. Excuses

Angela, a listener, wrote: *"I think that the reason some people hold onto being a victim is because they always have an excuse for their lives turning out like they do. It's scary to venture out and make changes and risk making mistakes and being responsible for your decisions. And if you act like someone else was in charge of your life and has control over your life, then you are not responsible for decisions or mistakes. You can blame them on someone else. And, you have the freedom to do whatever you like, even if it's not a good decision or hurts others."*

So many callers have lapsed into the "abuse excuse" in accepting the misbehaviors of others as well as their own.

Working with folks identifying as recovering damaged children, survivors, became such a huge moneymaking enterprise in the 1970s and 1980s. In order to feed that monster, it seemed that just about everything people felt or did was linked to some childhood trauma. It was hard to find anyone coming in for counseling with any other problem or perspective.

When I would ask an individual to speculate on some decision, reaction, or action, it was typical to hear, "low self-esteem . . . from abuse," "confusion . . . from abuse," "fears . . . from abuse," "reflexive emotions . . . from abuse," and so forth. And *that* would be where their insight would stop dead. It seemed enough to place the responsibility, not on themselves—on a lack of courage, compassion, or good sense—but on this nebulous thing called childhood trauma or abuse. They were satisfied that the causal relationship exonerated them from any further responsibility or culpability. It explained everything to them. Childhood trauma excused and relieved them from responsibility for the damage they'd do to themselves or others.

Excuses become a habit.

## 7. Avoid Challenges

Nobody expects much of suffering people. In fact, it seems cruel to demand accountability or responsibility from people who are mired in historical pain and misery.

I talk to husbands who don't know where to turn when their wives won't be sexually intimate with them because of childhood molestations. I talk to wives who don't know where to turn because their husbands are always angry because of childhood abuse. These husbands and wives have compassion, of course, but that compassion keeps them from demanding what should be part of intimacy: each person's most healthy and loving self. And that compassion keeps them starving for love and a healthy marriage.

"Damaged" people also avoid challenges (learning or trying new things), which may supply a painful failure—but also any success, which would cause them to have to leave their safety of their familiar, sad place of feeling bad for themselves and having the support of others.

Ashley, who had been there and done that, wrote: *"I think of a bad childhood as a deep hole; it is very hard to climb out of, but with hard work and a little help, it can be done. For me, the hardest thing was to relearn certain behaviors and defense mechanisms I learned as a child, such as crying to get what I want, horrible pessimism, feelings of not deserving my husband and children, a constant fear that 'the bottom was going to fall out' of something good, and trusting the people close to me.*

*"With God's grace and my husband's support I chose to work through and overcome those hurdles, and then I was able to work every day to have control over my life. It gets a little easier every day as my 'new life' becomes more and more comfortable. Now I am so glad that I made the choice to overcome my childhood and take control of my life."*

Of course, the biggest challenge is your resistance to overriding the programs in your head that keep you from your full potential as a human being.

Avoiding challenges is a means of keeping "safe." The irony is that the more "safe" you are, the less depth and texture there are to your life.

Avoiding challenges becomes a habit.

## 8. Center of the Universe

*"Abuse makes you very self-centered. Sexually and mentally abused from the age of three, my largest problem was no sense of self-worth, an attitude that I probably deserved to be hurt and that nobody cared. I became promiscuous and abused drugs and alcohol. I had a problem with all authority. I suffered with bitterness, resentment, anger, anxiety attacks and major depression. I lived in my feelings,"* explained Audrey, a listener.

Let's be honest: when your early life is basically one threat after another to your sanity or physical self, it's hard not to "live in your feelings." Unfortunately, that can get to be a way of life that precludes growth and joy, which generally come from attention to others than yourself.

More than just garnering attention is the childlike determination to be the Center of the Universe with just about everyone. This not only ensures perpetual caretaking, it also means that you don't have to tend to the needs or feelings of anyone else.

One recent caller, a young woman, was having trouble with her boyfriend. It seemed that every time he tried to talk to her about a problem in the relationship, she'd cry and he'd have to back off. He was getting frustrated, and she was worrying that he'd stop seeing her.

During our call I admonished her for sounding little-girl whiny. I asked her where she had learned to control and manipulate others with that behavior. At first she denied that motive. I persisted. She relented.

"My parents were divorced and it was hard to get attention from either one of them. They were busy being mad at each other and getting on with their own personal lives. But if I cried, sobbed, and was upset, they would drop everything, especially my dad, and take care of me. So, I guess I learned that by crying I could get them off their things onto me," she explained.

I told her that she was now using that to control her boyfriend. When he had concerns, complaints, or criticisms, whether about her or not, her crying brought out the chivalrous side of him and he gave up his position to caretake her. I asked her to think about that overnight, to discuss our conversation with her boyfriend, and to call me back the next day.

She did—or what seemed like some other woman did!

"I cannot believe how relieved I am to finally understand my so-called sensitivity. I've been manipulating him all along! That's how I got attention and things from my dad after their divorce. And when my boyfriend has any complaints about me I just turn on the tears and take back the spotlight. When I explained it to him last night, I felt so unburdened, so free. We are talking quite openly now and I've never felt closer to him. If there is a problem I want to hear it so that we can make it better. He is a wonderful guy and I don't want to lose him! Thank you, thank you."

I wish all transformations went that smoothly and quickly!

Men are quite different in how they become Center of the Universe. Men don't do it through tears of pain. Men are more likely to withdraw and drink or dominate and hurt with words or physical violence. In doing so, the entire family is constantly vigilant about his moods and afraid of "setting him off." He becomes the pampered, protected Center of the Universe because of his family's fears.

When I talk to these men on my radio program I always try to bring them to the point of understanding how their own historical pain (unloved) and fear of exposure (for that weakness or because of those horrible childhood "secrets"—like molestation) is impacting their ability to allow a woman to give them what any man needs—what they need but can't admit to, risk, or trust. I often recommend that they ask their woman for a hug—just to hold them and pet their hair. Believe it or not, that is excruciatingly difficult for many of these men to imagine doing. They've lived so long without tenderness, they've worked so hard to survive that loss by not needing it, they are so afraid of showing their vulnerability and being hurt or rejected again, that it is a monumental act of courage to simply say to their wives, "I'm sad, please hold me."

Oh, but when they do . . . it's a beautiful thing.

Being the Center of the Universe is a bad habit.

### 9. Change Is Scary/Hard

"*The worst legacy one lives with from childhood abuse is the ignorance on how to live a normal, balanced, healthy adult life! I had to learn, as an adult, how to behave in a mature way, how to be a wife, how to be a parent, how to take care of myself, how to handle stress, how to be stable,*" wrote Carol, a listener.

If you go to a bakery and see all the wonderful cakes and think it would be great to make one, but you have never even seen flour, milk, butter, sugar, salt, baking powder, chocolate, a spatula, a baking pan, or an oven—where would you start? You couldn't. You'd need someone to show you how. We all learn the tools and rules of living from our parents when we are children. When those lessons were warped, a sick parallel universe was created for you, one that does not allow you to prosper emotionally and interpersonally in this real world with everyone else. Your options and possibilities will appear severely constricted, and understandably, you flounder.

Cammi, another listener, wrote: *"Recognizing the kind of*

*life I want for myself and knowing that I will not get it by playing the perpetual victim role, which honestly, I did try that until age twenty-nine and it just didn't work, so I'm speaking from experience, sad to say. Gee, messing up my life was really exhausting!!"*

Once you have a notion of where you need to go and what you need to do to get there, it is still a difficult journey. What is familiar is comfortable, even when it is not healthy or rewarding. What is healthy and rewarding is unfamiliar, and thereby threatening and uncomfortable.

Cammi's grandfather (her mother's father) sexually abused her and viciously demeaned her dad without anyone ever saying or doing anything against him. Cammi ended up telling a neighbor. That infuriated her mom—no, not the molestation, but that a neighbor knew something "bad" about her father. No charges were ever filed, Mom made excuses for her dad, and the whole incident was swept under the rug as Grandpa stayed a part of their lives.

Consequently, Cammi didn't know the first thing about standing up for anything, even herself. Making herself feel better through excessive eating and bad guys worked, sort of, for a while. There was a little voice in the back of her mind that told her that she was out of control and she had to change. She went to therapy, really went to therapy to work hard, not just show up and whine for an hour.

*"I finally stood up for myself after years of just being angry, mad, and resentful and destroying myself in the process. You know, as crazy as this sounds, it's as though the adults in my life showed me that the molestation was OK, but I knew deep down inside that it wasn't, yet the way I dealt with that was by doing destructive things to myself."*

Cammi got to the point of no longer playing the blame game (her molestation is at fault) for *her* bad behaviors. This is a subtle and important point. Of course her family is to blame for her early victimization; her grandfather molested her, and her parents did not protect her or demand justice. But her family is not to blame for her choice of bad behaviors; her eating and promiscuity were her own decisions.

When Cammi told her mother and the rest of the family members that what they did was wrong and that they hurt her, she was correctly placing blame for *their* actions on their heads. She accepted the reality that her parents were weak and that they chose to be blind to evil. She accepted the fact that *they* were wrong, weak, and bad—not her.

Now she is a courageous person. She no longer just sucks up her emotions (and tons of food)—she deals with situations and people in an upfront, honest, brave manner.

*"We all have a past, some better than others, some worse than others. And, as children, we can't control what happens to us most of the time. But as adults, we can. For some, staying in pain keeps them safe from facing the wonderful opportunities that we have in life to grow. Growing requires getting out of the comfort zone* [even pain, if familiar, becomes a comfort zone], *which requires hard work, and let's face it—some people are just not up for the challenge."*

Joyce, a listener, best summarizes the difficulties involved in changing:

*"I struggle with my issues daily, and I have come to realize that they are as much a part of me as my smile, my eyes, and what kind of ice cream I like. With that, I see that I can choose to develop good habits, and even though I have been trained for twenty-nine years to react to situations negatively, FREEDOM comes when I can make a different choice.*

*"I have an amazing husband who helped me 'learn to love.' And I really believe love is a choice. That choice can change your bad mood, nag session, or your seemingly 'bad day.' So to all those out there who think it is too late to change, or that you have been at the*

*negative side for too long, I say baloney! I am living proof that God can change your life if you are willing to let him drive the rest of the way with you."*

Several years ago, when I first had the notion to write this book, I put a call out on my website for people to write to me about their Bad Childhoods, and how they got to a Good Life. I received many thousands of responses because the issue resonates on some level with just about everybody. I was interested to see the response to my question concerning what influence made the most positive difference in their lives. The number one answer was God and religion; the number two answer was some person who believed in them, stood by them, and demanded they be their best selves.

A woman whose alcoholic father was killed in a bar and whose manipulative and controlling mother was a perpetual "suicide" threatening to happen, wrote, *"Life is a series of choices, and the ones I have made, by the grace of God, have set me free. It has not been easy and there are still times I need to shove a tendency toward depression away—but with the help of God and my dear husband, success wins. I try to keep in mind that depression is a form of MEISM and that life is not just about me."* She signed herself "a blessed person."

When someone has been seriously hurt in their childhood, the defense mechanisms and manipulative patterns, the warped perceptions, the out-of-control emotions, and the hopelessness that results in depression/anxiety are tough to completely shed. The truth is that there is always a battle between history and the present. It takes patience, courage, and perseverance to stay with the healthier and more positive program. It is a lifelong battle. Some people, sadly, hug the security of the familiar and rue change.

Fear of change is a bad habit.

●     ●     ●

But change you must, if you hope to have a life with meaning, pleasure, peace, and joy. As Linda, a listener, observed:
*". . . you have to be ACTIVE in how you want your life to be—
letting your past run your life is like letting a caboose run a train. It
is just all behind you."*

Linda's attitude is correct and is confirmed by all the
people who struggle past their past, but it isn't easy. In the
next chapter, I will discuss the qualities necessary to move
toward that good life, and the difficulties along the road.

TWO

# Moving Toward the Good Life

*I was tired of being so angry and dysfunctional. It was time to let go and live my life the way it truly should be lived. I only wanted to be a happy person . . . Of course, I still struggle with it every day.*

**—Holly, a listener**

A Bad Childhood is easy to come by, and you don't have any control over that. A Good Life after a Bad Childhood is not easy to create, but you do have control over that. In a Bad Childhood you struggle against forces external to yourself. To come to a Good Life, the struggle is against forces internal—they *are* yourself.

## You're Kidding! I'm My Problem?

Angela called my program because she was obsessing about a boyfriend who rejected her a year before.

DR. LAURA: Getting dumped is very hurtful.
ANGELA: Yeah, so, um, I feel . . . he treated me . . . I let him

treat me really horribly and I feel like I know that it will never work and it's pointless to even think about him, but yet, I tend to want to ruminate . . .

DR. LAURA: When you ruminate, what are you thinking of?

ANGELA: Oh, gosh . . . um . . . like old good times that we had; things that we did.

DR. LAURA: So you whitewash it.

ANGELA: Yeah, yeah.

I then tried to get Angela to tell me why he dumped her. At first she only talked about how when they had problems in the relationship the way he dealt with it was to take off. He'd always come back. The question still remained as to why he dumped her permanently. She resisted answering this so hard that I knew there was something deep and dark inside her.

DR. LAURA: What do you think the reason was?

ANGELA: What do I think . . . um, I just . . .

DR. LAURA: Okay, Angela, let's try this. What's your worst fear that the reason was?

I had to ask her this question three times before she went inside herself for the answer.

ANGELA: (her voice got quiet) That I'm unlikable and horrible and nobody wants to be with me.

DR. LAURA: And where do you first think you got that notion?

ANGELA: From my upbringing.

DR. LAURA: And how did you get that notion from your upbringing?

Both of Angela's parents were alcoholic and critical. She described her mother as unstable and constantly telling her horrible things about herself. She said that her mom was a great mother when she was sober, so she would just sit around and wait for her to get sober. As a child, she never told anybody of her tumultuous home life until, at the age of twelve, she had to leave the home after her mother started to get more violent and, one day, pointed a gun at her.

The parallels between her relationship with her difficult mother from whom she took abuse and a difficult boyfriend from whom she took abuse are obvious. And it got worse. A social worker placed her with her father, who promptly dumped her into boarding school.

So her mother terrorized and demeaned her; her father got rid of her. Her worst fear is that her boyfriend dumped her because she is unlikable and horrible. Isn't that a reasonable conclusion of a child's mind, considering what her parents did?

DR. LAURA: Your worst fear is that your old boyfriend, as unloving and unstable as your mother, and as abandoning as your father, didn't want you because you must not be likable; and if your mother and father really didn't love and want you, why should anybody else? You are living your adult life with an assumption that both of your parents were correct. You've been working very had to convince a difficult, rejecting boyfriend to love you as a surrogate for finally attaining "mother love."

It can't work. Can you see how it's doomed from the start?

ANGELA: (quietly) Yeah, yeah.

DR. LAURA: Because if you pick bums, they're not going to love you, so you can never get what you want. You're wasting your life trying to make a "surrogate mother" come around. You could possibly do that until the day you die, unless you make a choice to do something different.

I clarified to Angela that her mother tortured her and her father abandoned her, and that made her a victim. But I explained to her that she was her own torturer and abandoner now.

DR. LAURA: Now, this is all you. You are repeating your history. You are doing it to yourself now. You are ensuring that you now are a victim. You were a nonconsensual victim when you were a kid—now you're volunteering yourself for victimhood!

Now that the schism between her emotions (tied into parental abuse and rejection) and her intelligence (awareness that her childhood hurt and loss could not be retread by re-forming a bum boyfriend) was clear in Angela's mind, the next question was...now what?

### Now What?

There are at least ten qualities that make it possible to liberate you from victimhood, and change your life from victim to victor.

### 1. A Look in the Mirror

Mirrors don't lie. Remember when the evil stepmother of Snow White asked, "Mirror, mirror on the wall, who is the fairest of them all?"? It ruined her day, but she got the truth. And so will you. It might ruin your day at first, but the truth, as they used to say in the 1960s, will set you free.

So look in the mirror and ask, "Mirror, mirror, on the wall, who is *now, today* the most injurious to me of them all?" Don't start arguing with the mirror when the answer comes back, "You!" I know you'll want to retort, "But my mother is so manipulative. My father is so controlling. My girl/boyfriend is so mean. Everybody let's me down and hurts my feelings! I can't help my feelings!"

Whew! Is that out of your system yet? No? Well, hang in there with me.

Does the notion of facing that the enemy of your serenity, functionality, and happiness is *inside yourself* make you angry because you feel more picked on by this seemingly further "blame"? I understand that reaction—it's reasonable. But if that's what you perceive as the bad news, here is the very good news: if your problem is what *you do* to yourself it means that *you* are the one with the *power* and the *control* and the *choice* to make it be different.

"*Throughout my teens*," wrote Wendy, a listener, "*and mid-20s, I made horrible choices: drugs, promiscuity, dropping out of college.*"

That is the mirror experience: Wendy admits s*he made horrible choices.* That is a very different mindset from "The Devil made me do it!" or "I just couldn't control myself" or "Bad things just seem to happen to me."

"*I was allowing*," she continued, "*my [childhood] experiences to dictate who I was, and I was not taking responsibility for who I was now.*"

The mirror told the truth: who Wendy was now was *her* responsibility, and *she'd* been misusing and abusing that power against herself.

"*I finally realized that I had a choice in the decisions I made, and that was very powerful. My life has changed drastically since then. Though I am not proud of my choices back then, I am grateful to develop such strength and character through adversity. I am no longer a victim.*"

Wait a moment! Does that imply that being a child victim is voluntary? No, definitely not. Having been victimized in one's childhood is a simple fact. Bad stuff happened to you when you were a defenseless, dependent child, or it did not. Fact. But here is the miracle, as I see it: **You are not a simple product of your experiences, you are a product of what you make of and do with those experiences.** Having *been* a victim as a child is not voluntary. Continuing to *be* an adult victim is voluntary.

That was a profound sentiment expressed in so many letters I received from listeners. Alana, a listener, offered: "*Will I choose to keep eating sour lemons, puckering my face in distaste, trying to figure out what I did to deserve the sour lemons? Or, should I dwell on how tasting sour lemons makes me feel? Or, make other people around me eat the sour lemons? Should I make eating sour lemons my habit, protesting that it is my only choice? Or, should I make lemonade? It may be easier to say it than do it, but regardless, it is a choice, and no one ever said that doing the right thing would always be easy. Simply, I choose.*"

As I discussed earlier and believe needs repeating because we are all somewhat blind to the bigger picture when our emotions are aroused, there is a straight-line connection between early childhood unhappiness or trauma and the self-destructive decisions we are making today. We don't always realize that we are basically attempting to repair yesterday by repetitively playing back that old home movie with today's characters, wondering all the while, "Why does this situation keep happening to me?" Since history cannot be changed, this is hopeless behavior. Nonetheless, people still have that pain. What becomes of it? Where does that pain go as you try to lead a good life and make strong, brave, healthy decisions?

The pain is always there, ever fading, like colorful fabric left out in the sun—but always there. Can we make something positive of it? Deborah has: "*I feel that at fifty, I am now where I should have been at age twenty-five. Hopefully, by the time I'm eighty, I'll finally feel grown up, can lose that little, lost child that still lurks inside me for good. She's there, and I probably still need her sometimes to remind me of how far I've come.*"

Deborah's positive view of that little lost child is that it is a marker from which she measures her growth. That is a wonderful reassignment of childhood pain.

Taking responsibility is liberating.

## 2. Enduring the Pain

Another listener revealed that "*While I've learned that I am a good person, to this day, when the boss calls me into his office, my first thought is 'What have I done wrong?' I still have problems making friends, but I'm trying: volunteering at school and church. I'm not afraid to make a decision, good or bad, and I've learned how to live with my failures.*"

Most people who call my program want to know the magic for making bad feelings totally and permanently disappear. Often they're angry or upset when I tell them there is no such magic. A good life is about *enduring*. That is generally not a popular answer. Our culture today of a pill for every ailment, physical or emotional, demands instant, simple, complete, permanent fixes. Real life just doesn't work that way.

Holly wrote of her struggles: "*One of the biggest struggles I still have is battling the self-esteem issue and having confidence to feel like I matter. It is definitely work, but I think anything worthwhile in life takes work.*"

Of course, it is easier to do the right thing when you're not fighting relentless messages from inside your head that:

- you're not worth much
- life is only about ugliness
- personal relationships are a threat
- effort and intent don't pay off because life isn't fair
- you could never be happy
- no one could love you
- nothing you try to do is any good
- life is pointless
- you're too damaged to get better or do better
- being good just makes you weak and vulnerable
- being vulnerable just means you'll be hurt

I've talked to too many people on the air for whom one or more of these thoughts had taken up permanent residence—stifling all possibilities of peace, happiness, and success in their lives. They believe that in order to move forward they must first eradicate those thoughts, pains, and fears. I let them know that they can't throw them out the car window—they have to drive with them lurking in the trunk.

It takes courage to forge ahead when your emotions tell you, "Danger! Don't bother! Nothing matters! You can't do it!" I liken the experience to taking a plane out of automatic pilot and flying manually; manual override means using your will, your intellect, your faith that there is more, different, and better out there for you and that you have to function by virtually ignoring the screaming negative signals from within yourself.

Don't wait for the pain to go away—it never will. However, you can challenge it with quality moments, experiences, and relationships. The pain will eventually have so many wonderful interruptions that it will become more readily tolerated and a less powerful force in your life.

Enduring is liberating.

### 3. Acceptance

I remember one woman in particular, in her fifties, whom I was counseling for various problems she was having in her life. This was an interesting case in that it seemed as though she was almost seeking out things to be hurt and upset about. She was a sweet and smart woman, very likable and competent. Yet, in an almost childlike manner, she kept looking for solace from her mother. When I tell you her mother was cold, critical, uninterested, emotionally remote, difficult, and self-centered, I am underplaying the reality. If there were ever a useless endeavor, it was this woman trying to get her mother to be solicitous, warm, supportive, interested, caring, or helpful.

When she came into session for the umpteenth time, hurt about her mother's disinterested and annoyed reaction to her calling about a problem, I told her that try as she might, she would never turn King Kong into a sock monkey; just wouldn't happen. I guess that imagery finally got the point across because her eyes opened unbelievably wide, and then she cried quietly for while.

She had spent her entire life trying to get her mother to act like one. And when it didn't happen, she tried some more. Maybe the next time would work? Maybe the next time her mother would be loving, and then she could feel good about herself? This ultimately useless, self-destructive, compulsive behavior kept her stuck as a disappointed child. "Am I supposed to not have anything to do with her?" she asked.

"I don't think that totally eliminating your mother from your life is going to fix anything," I replied. "In fact, I think it might make things worse because you might start obsessing about what she's thinking about you, and how you feel so incomplete and alone without some interaction with her. I think that you must accept who she is, what she can and cannot offer, and that you are not going to change anything about her or between you and your mother."

The concept of acceptance seems to be a difficult one. I define it as no longer fighting against something. It doesn't mean you embrace it or like it or agree with it. It simply (forgive that word) means that you won't fight it anymore. It is what it is, and now it is your turn to decide what you're going to do with it—or in spite of it.

I told this particular woman to call her mother up only to share something positive, or to ask her mother for some specific advice or opinion about something that was not emotionally charged, or to ask her mother about her day, job, or flower beds, or to simply make small talk.

It takes more moxie to adapt to reality (or accept it) than to avoid reality. In talking to her mother in a more adult manner, she will come to see herself as more of an adult, and interestingly, so will her mother. The dynamic will change dramatically, and in a healthier direction, without the need for some volatile confrontation or dramatic severing of the relationship.

Leah, a listener: *"I never felt like my parents\* heard me or understood how I felt. I have dealt with the reality of my childhood and have moved on to the adult life I choose to lead. I am very* *thankful for the positive traits I did get from my parents . . . I used to ask my mother to help me with whatever I was struggling with, and her standard response was a dismissive, 'I don't know, go figure it out.' Well, I want you to know that today, I am a successful sales person who figures most things out and never gives up until all avenues have been exhausted."*

Is acceptance a guarantee "slide on ice" toward a good life? No. It is always a struggle. Leah's letter went on to say that *"It feels comfortable to do things the wrong way. The struggle is ongoing. My life has been a series of challenges that I feel I would not have had so much trouble with had I had more guidance and understanding from my parents. My path has been a zigzag, but I made it. I feel that my common sense—and good sense—came from the hardships."*

Instead of trying to make her parents be more "parental" by screwing up and trying to force them to rescue and/or repair her, and instead of finding some parent surrogate to pick up their slack, Leah choose not to give in to the bad memories and blame that her sisters refused to let go of. She accepted the truth and limitations of her parents and committed herself to being, in a way, her own good parent.

Acceptance is liberating.

## 4. Letting Go

Holly, a listener, is thirty-seven years old. Her parents were divorced when she was two and her sister three. She and her sister were split up and each sent to a different set of

---

*Her father was a perpetual and blatant philanderer, while her mother was overwhelmed with six children. They instigated fights between the children, probably to deflect emotions away from themselves. They were never available to teach or support their kids because they were too absorbed in their own dramas.

grandparents to live with. At age seven, she moved back with her father and his new wife. Her sister stayed with the grandparents. Holly lived with a stepbrother, half-sister, and half-brother. Her father was physically violent.

*"When you are a kid,"* Holly wrote, *"this all seems normal and you really have no idea how it will affect you in later years. I always knew the way I felt shouldn't be how I was meant to feel, but I only realized all the effects of my childhood within the past couple of years.*

*"What really made it crystal clear were several conversations between my sister and me. It was quite obvious how angry and bitter she was. I realized that I felt the same way, but I didn't want to sound like this to other people and that I did not want to feel this way anymore. You can only blame your parents for so long. At some time in your life you need to take control and live a happy, normal life and not dwell on the past. It is not worth the pain and aggravation."*

Let me make something perfectly clear: the anger, disappointment, pain, and hurt you feel as a result of a Bad Childhood are righteous. You have been experiencing reasonable emotional responses to unreasonable experiences and circumstances.

That said, the human mind, body, and soul can only contemplate a limited number of issues at a time. What attention you put to bitterness takes away from the attention you can give to opera, hugging your child, learning something new, sailing, doing charitable work, being creative, feeling joy, and so forth. It comes down to a matter of quality of life.

When I suggest you "let it go," I do not mean you should "eat it," nor am I describing denial. Letting go means not allowing your bad thoughts, memories, and feelings from your Bad Childhood to squeeze out any joy you could enjoy in a Good Life.

Dale, a listener, wrote: "*My first marriage lasted twenty-three years and it should never have gone past two. I took a lot of rage out on the wife, like my father did on my mother. My next marriage lasted for fifteen years . . . I was older and a bit mellow, but still had a lot of MISDIRECTED ANGER. You can do whatever is necessary to succeed, no matter how angry or sad you are. Or, you can do as I did for a long time: have a great pity party for yourself, but then you discover nobody cares about you now either! It does take a lot of effort, and often I have wondered how much sadness and harm I have caused because of those circumstances.*

"*Although there is nothing I can do about the past, I now try to make each day as if it were the last. I have managed to engage in a serious, loving relationship these past three years, and she has promised to marry me this summer. ☺ And I said I would never marry again!*"

It is sobering to realize that your own personal pity party is a nasty double-edged sword. With your constant stirring-up of sadness and anger, on one edge you cut yourself up, and on the other edge you cut up other people . . . including the ones you love.

Lisa, a listener, wrote that she was never starved, raped, or burned with cigarettes in her childhood, which was, nonetheless, a very unhappy one. "*I seem to have turned out 'OK,' but I've done my share of messing up. When I'm wallowing in the past, I tend to mess up. When I'm looking toward the future, I do OK. The biggest challenge for all of us, regardless of how miserable our childhoods were, is to keep striding forward. My biggest personal challenge is to translate that from objective knowledge into personal daily experience.*

"*The best way I know to keep looking toward the future is to be the best possible mom I can be to my daughter, and that's what I try to do every day. Whether I feel lost or not, I'm her guide, and there would be no excuse for allowing her to feel lost with me. I get to break the chain. It's hard work."*

One of the main blind spots of people with a Bad Childhood is an inability to see how their "suffering" is impacting others—or sometimes an inability to care about how their suffering is impacting others. You might be so busy trying to deal with or remedy your past by your constant suffering over predictably bad parental relationships that you don't realize how much pain and loss your are causing your own children and spouse. Not only may you be behaving badly toward them directly (as with Dale and his misdirected anger), but your constant suffering or outrage over predictable slights, misunderstandings, disappointments, aggravations, and so forth brings a darkness into your home.

To one caller who complained about her ongoing problems with her "dysfunctional family," I said, "Madam, your complaints about your mother/father/whoever are reasonable. What is unreasonable is how much of your life is taken up in being sad, hurt, or angry about the stuff you *know* they're going to say and do. How much of this constant flow of aggravation do you express to your husband? How much of this constant flow of aggravation results in you not feeling up to being the best mother you can for your children? Companion to your friends? Friend to your neighbors? LET IT GO ALREADY!"

I work on these callers' sense of responsibility to their families to not bring constantly reprised dirty laundry into the home and spread it around the whole house. Of course you should bring issues up to your spouse to get help in coping. But that is largely not what is going on. What is happening is that you are using your family to pet you while you voluntarily let the fleas bite you—even soliciting bites by staying invested in the old bad dynamics of your dysfunctional family. You don't really want anti-flea medicine. You simply want your spouse to feel bad for you and slurp you up one side and down the other side for your pain. That is wrong, wrong, wrong, and selfish!

The imagery I've used on the air with people needing to let go, is for them to imagine all their frustrations and agonies of their Bad Childhood being pumped into a balloon—with an equal amount of helium. I tell them to wait until they're ready, and then let go of the string and watch the balloon lift away, eventually out of sight.

The response is usually one of some relief, but then a discomfort when they realize that they've got to hold onto something else. My suggestion is that they hold onto their own potential, the healthy love of friends and family, and a spiritual connection for guidance and solace.

Letting go is liberating.

### 5. Replacing Bad Habits

The problem created from experiencing a Bad Childhood is that you learned ways of thinking, feeling, reacting, and behaving in a context that is anything but constructive—and definitely shouldn't be generalized to the rest of your life. Nonetheless, it's what you learned, are familiar with and used to, and don't want to give up easily lest you feel naked and without powder in your bullets should you need to protect yourself again.

But it simply isn't rational or constructive to treat the world as though it were an instant replay of your childhood—and that's exactly what you do when you're:

- always suspicious of the motives of others and assuming the worst from them

- entering new situations with negativity, assuming the worst will happen to you

I believe that sometimes, consumed with confusing emotions and thoughts, you might find it extremely difficult to discern whether you're behaving in a way appropriate to the moment. Again, I call for manual override. One listener, familiar with the necessity of manually overriding such bad behavioral habits, wrote: *"It feels comfortable to do things the 'wrong' way. I consistently ask myself what the outcome of a decision might be, and if I am making it based on my childhood training or if it is a decision that I as an adult and in charge would be happy with. It is sometimes difficult not to slip into self-sabotage mode. Whenever I see myself going down a road that resembles where my parents have been, I usually recognize it and turn back."*

One of the most difficult aspects of a Good Life is just that ability to challenge yourself, frankly, the way I do to folks who call my radio program. People will call with problems and it is clear that they are *not thinking* any of their lives through at all—they are *just reacting* to all new experiences as though there were nothing new since their childhood—and I will challenge them to use logic. It probably feels uncomfortable and even brutal at times to the caller as well as the listener as I challenge them to face the fact that they themselves are:

- being cruel or annoying because they're scared of being hurt
- treating all men/women as though they were their own difficult father/mother
- cutting down on their own life's possibilities by allowing early negative perceptions of themselves to limit their efforts

- living in the past and avoiding the blessings of a better today and future
- being their own abuser now

I will force them to answer questions when they may want to cry, complain, explain, describe, excuse, and so on, like, "Is it your goal to be happy and have a life of peace and some purposeful accomplishment?"

"Yes, of course," is the usual answer.

"How does what you're doing contribute to that end?"

"Well, I guess it's not."

"Then why do or continue it?"

"I don't know, I guess it just happens to me and I don't know what to do instead."

"So, it's uncomfortable and scary to do anything but what you've been doing?"

"Yes."

"What do you think the solution is?"

"I guess that I'll have to get used to being uncomfortable and scared—I just don't know how to get better."

"It's funny, in a way, that you see taking risks to do 'healthy' things as painful, yet you've so much experience with pain that one would think you'd be more brave about it."

That is such an important realization. Why would somebody used to pain fear pain? A Good Life requires dealing with real pain even when you haven't had a Bad Childhood. Somehow that pain seems more intimidating and threatening than the old pain you're used to. Why? Same old answer: the familiar is comfortable even when it's ugly. New pains of loss, failure, disappointment, tragedies, betrayals, illnesses, and death have, in the minds of many with a Bad Childhood, the ability to prove your worst fear: your unworthiness; that your parents and your early perceptions were right! That fear is worse than recycling abuse, because then all hope would be lost.

The only way out is to take new risks and to remind yourself that bad things happen to good people, not just "bad children." *"I stumbled through several bad relationships, finally realizing how needy I was, how desperate I was, and it was being telegraphed to those scum who prey on women like I was,"* wrote a listener. She knew that she was the part of the picture that had to change because lightning was not striking the same place every few minutes—she was the lightning rod. Behaving differently would mean that she'd have to behave "as if" she were a catch, and risk the judgment and potential rejection of a "nice guy."

The core of growth and change is to risk challenging the negative perceptions from your childhood, behave "as if" you were valuable, and risk failure and rejection to prove the "as if" true!

As Michelle wrote: *"I had to learn that life is choice. I have so much control over most everything in my life. Get angry when I have to stand in line at the market or read a gossip magazine and be cool? Ditch my novel and give up, or send a query to yet another agent? Learn how to train my dog, or just figure I failed at dog ownership? Spend my afternoon looking up old boyfriends on the internet just for a cheap thrill, or be content and very happy with the great man I have?*

*"My brother is married to a nasty, foul-mouthed bully woman and is very unhappy. He refuses to take any control of his life. I understand how he feels, but he doesn't want to hear anything . . . change is too hard. His kids will suffer and carry on the legacy."*

Replacing bad habits is liberating.

## 6. Reach Out

People stuck in their Bad Childhood sometimes tend to reach out to others only to get affection, attention, capitulation, and approval, and won't necessarily desire to reciprocate. This is because the lack of love or peace in your childhood leaves you hungry, with an empty pit somewhere in your mind, gut, or heart to fill. The need to fill that space becomes neverending, like trying to fill up a bathtub that has holes in the bottom. Why? Trying to fill up a space that should have been filled by loving parents, an intact home, loving pats instead of violence, and so forth is complicated by the simultaneous, and impossible, fantasy that you will feel totally "healed," and the past repaired.

Over the years, I've explained to callers that "filling up" is a good and possible thing *only* when there is the recognition that the past stays a scar. Filling up is then about your present life with healthy, kind, encouraging, and supportive people and engaging in activities that are life-affirming. The former situation makes you a perpetual "taker"; the latter makes you a giving and loving human being.

Reaching out to others is a seriously important and necessary, although admittedly sometimes scary and risky action to take when you are working on having a Good Life. Most of the thousands of people who communicated their life stories to me in preparation for this book mentioned that there was someone who believed in them who made the difference between them staying lost or finding peace and happiness.

Many years ago, when I was in private practice, I was seeing a woman almost my age with a Bad Childhood. As an adult, she couldn't function well in intimate relationships with men, acted ditsy Marilyn Monroe–style, and was abusing drugs. After years of working with her on and off, realizing she had a good brain and supporting her going to college (she eventually became a nurse), giving her clothes from my closet so she'd have something to wear to work and school, giving her recommendations for jobs, when it was clear she was on a healthy track, I asked her what had happened in the therapy that made the biggest difference in her life. I guess I was egotistically looking for the brilliant intervention or incredible life-changing wisdom coming from me that was so powerfully "healing." I was more than humbled at her response—and I never forgot the profundity of its meaning: "You believed in me."

That was it, simple enough. "You believed in me." I remember being stunned. It was a tremendous learning lesson for me; technique was not the issue, humanity was. And she was right, I did believe in her. Frankly, I was amazed at the progress. I may have suggested school, but she's the one who faced down her demons to do it. I may have recommended her for employment, but she's the one who showed up every day and did her best job.

Because she respected me and I supported her, she came to believe in herself. If you think about it, that's what good parenting is supposed to do in the first place. You look up to your parents and when they are impressed and happy with you, you are then secure within yourself. When you never got that from them, there is an insecurity and lack of self-confidence that are difficult, but not impossible, to repair.

Another session with the same woman dealt with her anger that here she was, around forty years old, still struggling to grow up and accomplish something. She stormed around my office pointing at my diplomas, yelling that she was the same age as me and look where I was and look where she was.

I answered her by saying that "Yes, I'm more settled and focused in my life than you are. But I did not have to come out of the deep hole you had to climb out of. I don't know where I'd be if I had your hole to deal with. You can't compare us. You can only look at yourself with pride because many people just marinate in their respective holes. You didn't. You fought. You won. You're doing great. I'm proud of you. And you can't measure the progress of your life against mine unless we both had the same starting point. We didn't. And I don't know, we can never know, if I would have been as brave as you."

Misty, a listener, wrote, *"Once you make the decision to change, you have to be educated first on what the problem is and secondly how to fix it. Most people cannot do it entirely on their own. Which is why teachers, pastors, and mentors are so important. You can't change what you don't know. You can do anything if you knew someone believed in you and was there to encourage you. The kids in little league who have someone there cheering for them do much better."*

Kathleen grew up in a home with a "functioning" alcoholic father functioning meaning he owned his own successful business and kept a nice roof over the heads of his family. Unfortunately, with abuse of alcohol comes abuse of the children and spouse. Kathleen believes that she was blessed with the experience of being close to friends who had caring, loving families. She was able to see that there was a different way to run your life and be treated. She learned about love from those families. Kathleen wrote: *"I say your life will show up the way you run it. So, I CHOSE to run my life different than what I was taught at home, because of what I saw in a loving, caring family. Life is about CHOICES!*

*"I realized through relationships with 'normal' families that I*

*did not have a problem like my father would have me believe, but rather he was the problem. If I would have been isolated like many are in other abusive homes, and only saw the world according to my father, I probably would be really screwed up today."*

The bottom line is that you have to be willing to let people in to see you, really know you, advise you, support you, and even remind you when you're off track.

Reaching out is liberating.

### 7. Spirituality

One of the most insidious legacies of a Bad Childhood is the self-defensive posture created by the abuse or neglect. When you are constantly on the alert to making sure you won't be hurt again, the world becomes an unsafe place and the focus of your life is on how you feel; the center of the universe becomes "you."

As one listener wrote, *"We all have to be taught to love others. Children who are not taught this end up with hardened hearts and become very selfish. The saddest people in the world are the ones who put themselves first and don't care about others. They end up alone. These people end up bad because they don't care who they hurt."*

Healthy families teach children about being compassionate and loving toward others, primarily by how they treat each other, the parental relationship being especially important. It scares me how often a husband/father or wife/mother will call and tell me that their kids are not being abused or upset because the bad behavior is just between the adults. They are kidding themselves. Ever see one of those commercials where the husband and wife are being sweet to each other, and their small child is peeking at this idyllic scene? The child is always in heaven, buoyed by their love and content in its reflection. Well, the converse is also true; when parents are cruel and disdainful of each other, children are in hell, undermined by their hate and damaged by its backwash.

This self-focus is about suffering: spiritual and emotional hunger, self-defense, fears, discomforts, as well as a poorly formed sense of one's purpose in life.

For many emotionally shell-shocked people, one's purpose in life becomes telescoped into issues of survival. I have challenged such callers to my radio program to tell me what the ultimate purpose is of their existence. At first they are shocked, not quite imagining that there is some sort of "cosmic assignment" that they're late in handing in. I insist that there is; that they have certain talents, abilities, potential, and missions in this world—all of which is being set aside while they lick their emotional wounds.

One listener wrote that she was having a conversation with another child with an alcoholic parent who told her that she'd had a conversation with her own thirty-year-old brother who blamed every failure on their father—as though the father's drinking had ruined any possibility or hope for a decent life for himself. Her reply to her brother was, "That was the first eighteen years of your life; now what are you going to do with the rest of it?"

This is exactly one of the reasons why I am so cautious about suggesting therapy to people angry and hurt with their childhoods. Too much of mainstream psychotherapy focuses in on the pain and rage and the past, week after week after week. I have told people on the air that they were talking about and analyzing themselves so much that their world was so constricted that they couldn't see beauty and hope, nor could they see the damage they were doing to others, not only through neglect, but through the sense of entitlement that comes from imagining that your pain makes you special and most important in any relationship.

I would more likely suggest that they pray. That usually gets me a snort from the caller. I point out that pain, fear, injustice, cruelty, and disappointment are eternal, universal realities of the human experience, not just their own sad possessions. And since we cannot ever have back that which we've once lost—a good childhood—we are left with only two alternatives: the first, to stay in the past for the rest of our lives; the second, to determine to be a beautiful sunrise to the lives of others.

Note that the second alternative is outward-reaching. That's important. The best cure for sadness is to be the means by which sadness is taken away from someone else. This is the primary function of religious instruction: to teach you that you are part of something bigger than yourself, and that you matter by virtue of what you bring to others and to the world. The focus of spiritual training is outward, not inward. Inward focus is akin to mildew. Outward focus is akin to a breath of fresh air.

Spirituality is about opening outward. No, it doesn't erase the past, nor heal all your wounds. But then, nothing can do that. You can, however, decide that this, being the first day of the rest of your life, is your opportunity to *be* the loving spirit that you wish you had in your own life. Living for something or someone outside of yourself is the primary means by which we all find purpose and value in our lives.

Spirituality is liberating.

### 8. Perspective

*"I had to share with you that having been to India twice in the last five years makes you realize that nothing could be as bad as that! So, in a nutshell, I think it's a thing of counting your blessings every day. Of course, some people can't find the way out as 'easy' as*

*I did . . . but I say, give them a mirror, a padded room, and let them think about it for a while. I know it sounds simple, but heck, it worked for me."*

That letter was written to me by a woman who described herself as a wreck, emotionally and psychologically, from her childhood with a very sick set of parents. She realized she had tons of problems related to that upbringing and finally committed herself to a mental hospital in Holland, where she grew up.

*"In Holland, you have to commit yourself and you have twelve weeks to figure out what needs to be done while in a psychiatric hospital wing before you are shipped to a 'closed facility.' I did it in ten weeks. It was almost a 'let go and let God' type of thing . . . best time of my life, by the way. Worked really hard with two psychiatrists, and finally understood that if I couldn't commit suicide, I might as well enjoy the ride . . . hence . . . I've had a terrific time since.*

*"I count my blessings every day and abhor the people who maintain their victim status."*

Experiences of perspective are those that take you off your personal victim island and put you in the world with the rest of humankind. Not only can you then see options with respect to giving and participating in that larger world, but I hope you can also see how you are wasting precious life time by continuing to fuss over yesterday and not taking advantage of the opportunities you have for happiness now and forever.

This is exactly why I nag people still suffering from Bad Childhoods to get involved in volunteer work, charitable causes, peer support in hospices, anything where they get to see that suffering is a universal experience, and anything where they get to feel the pleasure of bringing peace to someone else—which is exhilarating.

Perspective also means that you can, without denial or whitewashing your past or your difficult or dangerous family members, pick out those things that were valuable or benevolent. I have spent a lot of time convincing people to look at the flower petals, and not just the thorns, dirt, worms, and fertilizer. When a caller complains that they were abandoned by their parents and brought up by a foster care family or other relatives, I talk to them about the blessing of being rescued by people who turned their lives around to be there for them.

When a young woman calls about her sadness that at her wedding her father, who abandoned her eons ago, will not be there to walk her down the aisle, I remind her of the blessing of a stepfather who stepped up to the plate and volunteered to take care of her lovingly and responsibly.

When a man calls about his anger with his abusive mother, I point out that now he has a woman, a wife, who loves him and is patient with his self-indulgent suffering over the past. I remind him that his behavior could drive her nuts enough that she might start behaving like his mother, and that maybe a better solution would be to relax and enjoy the product of his healthy side in picking a good woman.

Basically, when people call stuck in victim mode, I remind them that they are alive, and that is the biggest blessing of all, because that gives them time to *finally* be happy.

Perspective is liberating.

### 9. Hobbies

I bet you think this topic is silly and misplaced in a list of such profound concepts. Well, that may be precisely your problem! Constantly being sad, mopey, angry, hurt, and anticipating more situations to be such is not only negative, it's exhausting! And feeling bad perpetuates more feeling bad. I realize that some people resist feeling good because they are gripping their victim status tightly, lest they be held to a higher standard of existence by those around them, and then what would happen to all their "damaged person"—generated attention, affection, approval—and special dispensation from reciprocation and responsibility? But it is a truism that feeling good breeds more feeling good.

Distractions are good, and hobbies are an opportunity to move your mind away from somber issues into an arena of creativity, constructive activity, positive growth and change, discovery and new knowledge, a sense of competency, exciting challenges, new friends—and possibly a whole new perspective on life's possibilities.

Probably one of the most benevolent things I have done for myself is to take up sailing. When we moved to an area by the ocean, I decided to get a small powerboat just to tear around in. At the last minute, I thought I might take one sailing lesson just to see what it's like, but I was convinced it wouldn't be for me—that next to the speed from the double engines of a powerboat, it would just be too slow! I was out on the water for only twenty minutes with my instructor, Helene Webb, who already had me steering and running the mainsheet (yikes!) when I realized the beauty of the wind in the sails and on my face. I was just amazed at the feeling of quietly moving through the water with just the wind to propel me. To then make a turn (gybe, tack) around a bell buoy with about a dozen sea lions piled up grabbed me for life. I immediately signed up for the beginner's keelboat course and now, two years later, have a ton of trophies for racing—but, more importantly, I have been moved by the serenity and challenge of being out on the water, dealing with the currents and winds.

Whenever I feel sad, overwhelmed, negative, frustrated,

angry . . . I just go out on the ocean and my mind and soul are cleansed.

Hobbies are liberating.

## 10. Attitude

I remember watching a television documentary on Third World countries. The interviewer came up to this incredibly old man, all skin and bones, crouched down on his meager haunches, holding a staff in one hand for balance, gesturing with the other as he spoke with a huge grin revealing very few teeth. The interviewer asked him if he was happy. This seemingly pathetic old man said incredibly, "Yes." The interviewer asked him, "How can you be happy? You have a hut for a home, little food, no possessions to speak of. How can you be happy?" The old man smiled again as he said something like, "I am alive to share time with friends and family."

That was that.

And just in case you haven't heard this one: A grandpa is talking to his grandson about the two wolves that occupy his head. One wolf is bitter, angry, resentful, hypersensitive, and even bites his own paws. The other wolf is content, kind, open, caretaking, cooperative, and friendly. "These two wolves are constantly fighting." Alarmed, the grandson asked, "Who is going to win, Grandpa?"

"The one I feed."

A positive attitude is liberating.

THREE

# Closure Versus Resilience

*Life is not fair! Life is not easy! There is no rulebook or secret to success or happiness. Happiness is earned and sustained through character and strength. God creates miracles for us to have if we are smart enough to realize them.*

**—an anonymous listener**

*I hate the word closure!*

**—Carole, a listener**

In the 1980s the concept of "trauma" became an official diagnosis, and research and treatment were focused on the supposed benefits of "talking it out" and "facing it down." Obviously, the folks who are resilient (suffer, endure, move on) don't come into therapists' offices, nor do they volunteer for research projects on suffering from an acute or childhood trauma. So all the emphasis has always been on dysfunction, without equivalent attention given to learning from those who cope—who are the majority. It seems that we could learn more about helping people who are suffering from past traumas from the struggles and actions of those who have prevailed without an inordinate duration of personal suffering or derailment from their life's path, and without intensive "professional" intervention. That is what I offer you in this chapter.

Since about 1995, when the term "closure" was first introduced, the counseling industry grabbed this concept tightly, threatening and promising that you would never be able to be happy and function well in life without bringing your emotional history to a satisfactory conclusion, aka closure. This closure required lengthy examination of your history of abuse or disappointment and perhaps years of therapy, not to mention a confrontation or three with whoever contributed to your hurtful past. Folks who say they were getting on with life satisfactorily without these efforts are said to be in denial, minimizing their issues, avoidant, and distracting themselves from their real problems. The threat is that if these so-called "repressive" behaviors continue, they will cause you to emotionally erupt at some point and spew destructive psychological lava in all directions.

If after closure therapy you still had painful thoughts from childhood, or had to struggle against your inner, pouty, or angry self, it was then clear that closure hadn't occurred and you should be back in the bowels of the multimillion-dollar therapy recovery/trauma therapy industry.

At the risk of getting ahead of myself, let me state here that generally, going back over and over the memories of trauma will likely get you sicker and sicker—as too many of you have probably learned by now. Also, I have long worried about what I've seen as a societal and mental health world *pressure to be sick* because of some experience, or to label oneself a victim of "something" from your childhood. Let's face it, from childhood we learned that if you have a stomachache you won't have to go to school, won't have to do your chores, and will get lots of solicitous attention. There is a payoff to being "sick" or unhappy.

Certainly, the psychotherapeutic world went crazy in the 1980s diagnosing just about every woman with emotional problems as being a victim of molestation whether they remembered it or not; hence the now-debunked Repressed Memory Syndrome. The hysterical, toxic, feminist "all women are victims" agenda forced women to see themselves as traumatized and victimized, even if they had a minor event that they probably could just put on a mental shelf and get on with life.

Some people, like Julie, a listener, resisted these sometimes well-meaning but destructive pressures. In Julie's letter to me, she described herself as the adult in her family, consisting of a drunk father, a depressed/suicidal mother, and an older brother who ignored the whole situation. When Julie was nine years old, her mother asked her what she should do about her dad and the whole family. She told her mother that she thought Mom should get Dad out of the house because they were all miserable and not safe. Her mother yelled at her and didn't talk to her for days, probably because the thought of taking control and responsibility was far too frightening and she was too weak.

When Julie was sixteen, her mother finally got her backbone fused properly and left that violent home. Julie and her brother worked to help support the three of them. She remembers actually having some "normal" family moments.

*"I decided,"* Julie wrote, *"that I was not going to let my childhood rule the woman I was to become. I was polite to my father when he called on my birthday every year (the only time he ever called), but other than that I really didn't think about him. I went*

*into the medical support field and found myself surrounded by nurses, social workers and psychologists, who, as we became friendly, told me I need to 'have closure' with my father and that I would never be alright until I 'confronted' him about my childhood."*

Fortunately, Julie trusted her own instincts and didn't sign up for that confrontation. Instead, to whoever challenged her, she expressed loving her father for giving her life and for being her hero when she was very small, but believed that she had to close that part of her life in order to turn all her energies into her family as an adult.

*"I had an awful time trying to explain to my well-meaning friends and family that just because one decides to eliminate someone out of their lives, that doesn't mean that there are bad feelings that need to be dealt with. It simply means that I decided to leave the pain in the past."*

Unfortunately, conventional wisdom in the psychotherapeutic arena has held, for the last twenty or so years, that people who experienced ugliness in their childhood, or who were unnecessarily traumatized by any life experience, had to talk it over and over and over to overcome. Adults abused as children had to not only talk it over and over and over, they had to formally confront their wrongdoer and "let 'em have it" with a repeat of history and a blaming for the pain and difficulties and struggles they still have. I believe that in the vast majority of circumstances, outside of issues of legal justice, this is more injurious than healing.

The notion was, and largely still is, that one cannot move on in life until closure occurs, as though closure were some sort of screwcap trapping your inner pain in a bottle, away from your current life.

The very term *closure,* implies an endpoint, a cessation. I get so many calls with folks telling me that they want the thoughts, feelings, and memories to go away. "You know," they say to me, "closure." They become very frustrated when I tell them that there is no such thing as their history being erased or made entirely powerless unless I scoop out significant portions of their cerebral cortex, or they are stoned or drunk all the time, or they're in a coma, or they make such a crazy life that they have no time to ruminate.

Chuck called my radio show, very subdued, telling me that he could no longer stand the negativity he had in his head about life and about himself. He was in his early thirties, married to a good woman, and had three children he loved.

DR. LAURA: So, Chuck, you're one of those folks who anguishes over what isn't in his half-filled cup, while others revel and celebrate what is in their half-filled cup?

CHUCK: Yeah. I just can't help it. Negative thoughts come into my mind, followed by negative feelings. I had a lot of abuse in my childhood.

DR. LAURA: (intentionally not commenting on the abuse) Yes, you're right, negative thoughts and memories happily invite negative feelings to join them for cocktails. No question about that. But you can do something about that each and every time it happens!

CHUCK: How?

DR. LAURA: Well, it seems to me with your health being good, your job being successful, your wife being nice, your three children being fun . . . you've got a lot to tap into. Am I correct in those assumptions?

CHUCK: Yes, but I'm still negative—even being aware of the good things.

DR. LAURA: Okay, Chuck, close your eyes and see yourself in bed with your wife, feel her soft skin against yours, and get into the feelings of rapture when you're making love. Tell me when you're there.

CHUCK: There.

DR. LAURA: Is it wonderful?

CHUCK (with enthusiasm): Oh yes!

DR. LAURA: Okay, Chuck, now close your eyes and put yourself put yourself back in that horrible place from your childhood which you still suffer from. Do not tell me what it is—just tell me when you're there.

CHUCK: (moments of silence and then a strained voice): There.

DR. LAURA: Now I want you to shift your attention, keep your eyes closed, go back to the scene in your life today, making love to your wife, the smooth texture of her skin, the love in her lips. Can you hold onto the bad images and feelings when you do that?

CHUCK: No, I can't. So, you're saying that I have to make a conscious effort? I have to break the habit of staying with the thoughts when they pop back into my mind?

DR. LAURA: You're sounding like that's a bad thing. Chuck, you have the power to shift your thoughts out of the ugly past into the beautiful present you have built. You have that power.

This very moment was the turning point for Chuck—and probably for many other listeners identifying with him. When I said "power," I hit the core issue for people having trouble moving away from the emotional consequences of their traumatic childhoods: the sense of powerlessness, and impotency, the inability to protest or protect themselves.

CHUCK: Oh my god! Power! That's amazing. You know, I've always felt that I was powerless because of what happened to me as a kid. Feeling powerless is at the center of my pain—it's been my problem.

DR. LAURA: You were powerless then—as a child; you're not powerless now, as an adult. You have the power of will to take the beauty in your life today and use that to overwhelm the thoughts and memories from yesterday. You can't be in two places at once in your mind—and Chuck, you get to choose. You have the power!

Chuck's attitude, in the space of the three or four minutes we had together on the air, went from defeated to commanding. Please notice that I never had to hear the specifics about "what happened," because no matter how he came into that hole, and no matter what was in that hole with him, there was only one way out: his power to instantaneously replace the bad feelings, and memories of the past, with the lovely ones of his present.

To those of you who think you don't have positive feelings and thoughts to use as replacements for habitual, familiar bad and sad memories, I have three things to say: (1) make better choices and build them, (2) look harder, they're there, and (3) good feelings will become more comfortable and addictive, I promise.

This experience with Chuck is the best example I have of what closure really is. There is no end to your awareness of painful feelings and the memories that spawn them, but there is a likely end to those feelings and memories overwhelming you into a sense of hopelessness. You and Chuck now have a very important tool in the inner war against old enemies: *your will* to happiness and peace. Your will to not be the *slave*, but the *master* of your life *now*, is your key to the chains locking you into your miserable past.

No one can give you peace. It is a gift you give yourself.

A friend of mine who seems to know a lot of people with particularly sad histories e-mailed me that she was really looking forward to this book, hoping to understand why some of her friends wallowed and others paddled. That is a good question. Why would anyone choose not to use their power to have a good life? I believe it comes down to the ten factors below, some of which I expanded upon in Chapter 1. I believe it is important to nag you about these factors because you'll have to confront each one in order to allow your own resilience to flourish.

1. *Fear* is the dominant mind-set (what if all people will hurt you, and what the abusers said about you, or made you feel about yourself, *is* true?)
2. *Ignorance* of your inherent power to make things today be different
3. *Character* weaknesses (lack of grit and will)
4. *Isolation* from support (self-protective distance)
5. *Habitual lifestyle* (the familiar, ugly as it is, is comfortable, and you deal with it—all change provokes anxiety)
6. *Secondary gains* (because of being "in pain," you have control over others, manipulate through guilt, and excuse yourself from responsibilities)
7. *Identity* (you are only what you suffered through)
8. *Self-centeredness* (your relationships and experiences are all circumscribed around how you feel/are impacted)
9. *Negative thinking* (no celebration of what *is* half-filling your cup)
10. *Laziness* (simply not hunkering down and "doing it")

Any one person may be shuffling all or only some of these cards in their hands. One woman called me recently complaining that she didn't know why she couldn't get intimate with her boyfriend. I had to struggle with her to find out if she meant sexually, personally, or both. We settled on half and half. She was in her early thirties, had never (#5) kept a long-term relationship (#4), because, she said, "I'm scared (#1) of something and I don't know what."

I suggested that she might be scared of finding out that her worst fear was true, that because her parent(s) were unloving or abusive that it meant she was unworthy (#7) of love. "Is your definition of intimacy that the man, or a friend, will find out things about you that are less than admirable and that you won't be loved? In fact, you'll be judged negatively and rejected? So, to keep yourself safe from that potential pain, you never let them see you? Basically, you play it safe?" (#3, #10)

She answered yes.

"Do you realize that *all human beings,* regardless of their childhoods, fear the exact same thing? Do you realize that everybody wants to be accepted, admired, and loved? Do you realize that the most devastating experience for every human being is rejection and abandonment? Do you realize that this reality is not just your private possession because of your painful past?"

"No, I never thought about it that way." (#2)

"Well, my dear, you're going to have to suffer the same risks, losses, gains, failures, and successes the rest of us fellow human beings have to confront. Ten years of therapy will not excuse you from the natural laws of physics: risk brings a mixture of triumphs and sometimes failures. That's just the way it is! You're going to have to take risks with the rest of us. That's the gut and grit part of life."

She came back with, "Oy, risks. Yes, I guess that's right. I've been avoiding taking risks." (#3)

"Not only that—but when you keep 'safe' by keeping a distance emotionally and physically, you are doing to your boyfriend the very exact thing you don't want to experience: rejection!" (#6)

"I didn't even see it that way."

"And furthermore," I continued, "Do you realize that you are the most self-centered person in your own life?" (#6, #8)

She answered, "That's exactly what my boyfriend said to me last night. Oh my gosh, I never wanted to see myself that way!"

"Hey, woman, you have a man who is hanging in there with you, don't blow it." (#9)

I went on to explain to her that what makes us connect to others, what increases our chances of being admired, appreciated, and loved and makes our lives meaningful and happy, is being centered on what we have to offer someone else! In fact, I invited her to sing, "me, me, me, me, me," with me for about five seconds. I then told her to hang up and start singing, "you, you, you, you," and call me back in a week. See? Therapy can be fun!

## Your Life from the Rearview Mirror

Another anonymous listener wrote about her "search for closure": "*I used to think that 'closure' was important, but the older I have gotten, the more I realize that simply* letting go *and going on with my life was my best option. The search for closure causes too much self-focus on the wrong things, and not on options and potential.*

"*It is such a waste of time to look through that rear view mirror while driving forward in life, and I would encourage others to stop looking at their scars and start nurturing the part of them that is healthy, despite a horrible childhood.*

*"Why have I been more successful than my siblings? I don't know. We were all raised in the same hell. I could go on and on about the circumstances. I also can tell you, Dr. Laura, that it would have been SO MUCH EASIER for me to drink my life away and feel sorry for myself. I made a decision long ago that my life had more to offer me."*

A decision? A decision not to ruminate and suffer? A decision to limit the negative impact of traumatic early life experiences on your ability to love life today? A decision?

It would seem that for most people, it is all about a decision: *"My brother and I both chose routes that were detrimental to our well-being, and my brother, now thirty-one, is in prison as he chose the route of lashing out criminally. When I was fourteen, I did as most girls do who didn't have fathers, and whose mothers were mean and degrading, and started looking for love in places I would never find it, smoking pot and drinking regularly, and at fifteen I was pregnant with my daughter. At seventeen I was pregnant again and this one I gave up for adoption, knowing I couldn't provide a good life for two children.*

*"Then I met the man of my dreams and got married at twenty; six years later we are still married. We have my daughter who is now ten, who doesn't have a clue that she's the product of teenage promiscuity since my husband accepted her from the moment he met her and even adopted her a year after we married.*

*"The point I am trying to make is that I hope many women who call your show and feel worthless because of how they were raised take your advice. Because of all the circumstances in my life, if I lived how some of the 'pop psychology' say, I would be down on myself all of the time, blaming my father and mother for all my problems, and not providing a good life to my children and husband. I don't use the divorce, the rapes, the beatings, the shack-ups, the mother who could care less or anything else to justify anything other*

*than it made me stronger, and I know now that I have a good life in
spite of it all."*

Understandably, some people have a tough time making
that decision. I received a phone call from Julie, whose husband
of six years has always had an on-again, off-again relationship
with his mother, who has been diagnosed with mental problems. When I asked what made it "off again," Julie told me that
when she got upset about something she stopped calling and
talking. The "something" is his mother's feeling that he didn't
call or come over enough. In short, he wasn't giving her
enough attention. Julie said that it had been difficult for her
husband and his brother to grow up with a mother who would
be so sensitive and punitive.

Her question for me concerned that fact that he and his
mother hadn't spoken in a year, and she continues, however,
to send holiday cards, birthday cards, and anniversary cards
through the mail.

I said, which went unnoticed, "That is nice."

Julie kept on going: "When she does that it makes my
husband upset because it stirs up all that emotion."

"Julie, you have to tell your husband that at this point in
his life he has to accept that this is the best his mother can
do. He has to learn to enjoy the gift of the cards, without
using each of these cards as a trigger for mourning what he
didn't and doesn't have in a warm, mushy mother. Getting
the cards is better than not getting the cards. Tell him not to
discount the plate of spaghetti because it's fifty strands wanting. This is the best she can do."

"Dr. Laura, should he pick up the phone and call her?"

"Sure, to say 'Thank you' for the card. And accept that that's
his mother, and she's limited. This is probably one of the most
important things people have to learn about their 'difficult'

parental situations. She's not evil, she's annoying, she's tortured within her own mind. She's more comfortable sending cards than actually interacting. This is the best she can do. She's probably not intending to hurt him—she's all focused in on her hurts. She is a limited human being—and suffering herself.

"Your husband has to grow up a little bit, and get perspective about the fifty strands of spaghetti he does have. He has to be able to go to the mailbox and say, 'That's nice, at least she sent a card.' He has to be able to say that or *he* is ruining his adult time—not her. She's a predictable constant. Your husband has to acknowledge to himself that she's not going to morph into Supermom, but he can emotionally distance his immediate well-being from her predictable behaviors."

Another listener wrote to me with profound admiration for her husband's handling of his childhood pain due to his horrendous mothering: " . . . *because if I were to tell you what kind of childhood he had, you would have guessed he turned out to be a deadbeat father, drug addict, and loser. The thing I find the most amazing is how my husband turned out. My husband never spends a second feeling sorry for himself. He does look in the past, but not to dwell on the negative, but to take from it a learning experience and something to grow on. He looks at his childhood as an example of what he doesn't want out of life.*

*"I'm amazed that he even knows how to love. He has chosen to be polite and nice around his mother, but has opted to lead a completely separate life, surrounding himself with good and decent people."*

I just know that this latter gentleman would probably, by the yardstick of today's psychotherapeutic environment, be labeled as repressed, in denial, with the potential of exploding (into drug or alcohol abuse, mental illness, violence) when it all eventually erupts to the surface. The factors that speak against that so-called inevitability are that he:

- isn't hiding anything from himself, having acknowledged and accepted the painful, ugly truth of his Bad Childhood experiences, in contrast to denying the experiences or whitewashing the abusers
- likely has an awareness of his vulnerable points, which are a product of his early experiences, and doesn't let them rule his life or command his behaviors
- made the connection between the trauma of his childhood and his inappropriate, unconstructive behaviors and reflexive thought and feeling processes of today—and stays on top of it
- accepts that the demons wiggle their tails in his gut sometimes, but that he can survive that without thinking that he's not okay
- made life choices that are fulfilling, exhilarating, and satisfying
- is part of a healthy family that he's helped create that supports and nurtures him

That's not the pattern of a person who is going to erupt in anything but a better life than he came from.

## Yeah, but What About an Apology?

Some of you are convinced that you can't—or won't—get on with your life in a more satisfying way until you get either an acknowledgment or an apology from the parties that hurt you. Obviously, there is an inherent problem in this equation if they are dead or they haven't changed a molecule of their being!

Nonetheless, when we're kids and have a fight and our parents made us shake hands and say, "Sorry," we usually let go of the rage and got on with being friends. I think that because of those many benevolent experiences, you think the same thing should happen as an adult. It generally doesn't, even when the apology is sincere. Why? Because, as opposed to the few minutes or hours between misdeed and apologies when you were a kid, the impact of a Bad Childhood spreads over years, even decades, during the time when your sense of personal worth; perspective on hope, life, and possibilities; ability to trust and risk; and a belief in God and love were all forming. There is, literally, too much that's happened to make an apology change much of anything—really.

Miriam, a listener, wrote to me about apologies: "*In 1984, when my father, who had molested me from the age of 4 until I was around 13 or 14, was dying from cancer, I confronted him. I accused him of ruining my life (at the time I was 34 years old) and was headed toward alcoholism, promiscuity, and being a deadbeat when it came to paying bills, etc. Anyway, my father said that he did not ruin my life, and that I was using him as an excuse to continue screwing up.*

"*On my plane trip back home, I thought about what he said. He never denied hurting me and he never said he was sorry, but he did give me reason to think. And, as much as I hated to agree with him—I was blaming him for all the mistakes I had made.*

"*It is difficult to do, but I have to give my father credit for making a turning point for me. I realized that I do have control of my life. I stopped going into bars, started parenting my son, and started paying my bills. I still have a problem sometimes keeping my bills paid. I still suffer from depression, and spending money seems to help. I do not drink which eliminated the promiscuity. Sometimes I cannot shake the cloud hanging over me. . . . what happened on his death bed saved my life.*" *

*She says she has siblings, all of whom are still drug users, alcoholics, overeaters, multiply divorced, and generally unhappy.

Miriam did not get her apology. In fact, you could say that her father blamed her whole life on her—yet another form of abuse? Perhaps, in a way, but she was called by her abuser, ironically, to face the fact that getting off track and staying off track are the results of two separate forces. Her father's evil got her and her siblings off track; after that, she was the sole conductor of her at times rickety train.

The question remains as to whether a person deeply damaged by a Bad Childhood can ever really have a Good Life. The answer is definitely "yes," with a caveat: if a good life can be portrayed as a slice of cheese, some people's lives might be more like American, and others more like Swiss, with some holes. Nonetheless, it is all cheese—which is better than soupy, goopy, bitter curd.

Gina wrote that she can *". . . certainly empathize with those that have grown up with an abusive, dysfunctional start to their lives. I have been where they are. It does no good to dwell on the pain, because the past is past.*

*"There is nothing that can be done to change it. You can't make abusers apologize, and even if you could, the apology does not change what they did. The change has to come from within the person who has been abused. That is the bottom line. You must make a decision to move on, let it go and live."*

Mark, a forty-two-year-old man, married eighteen years to a wonderful woman with two beautiful kids, a daughter seventeen years old and a son fifteen, called about still having unresolved issues about his father, who hadn't come into his life until he was sixteen.

MARK: Whenever he pats me on the back when we get together for the holidays, I just cringe when he touches me. Am I wrong to feel this way?

DR. LAURA: What is the unresolved issue?

MARK: Well, I guess just the fact of him not being around at all until I was sixteen.

DR. LAURA: Sir, how do you imagine you're going to resolve that issue?

MARK: I've tried talking to him about it.

DR. LAURA: But Mark, how are you going to ever resolve history?

MARK: I guess you're right.

DR. LAURA: What can he say or do that makes the years between birth and sixteen any different?

MARK: I don't know. I guess an "I'm sorry" would be a start.

DR. LAURA: If you believe that, simply say, 'Dad, I need you to say you're sorry.' You have to have the courage to say that and not be phony at Christmas and Thanksgiving, and then cringe under your own lack of willingness to be honest. I suppose that's because you don't want to be rejected or abandoned twice! Just remember, it really won't change anything about history but it might make you feel better right now to see him accept some responsibility for having done damage. But Mark, it might not make you comfortable with his touching you. That comfort level will only develop through time. An apology is not about yesterday, it's about a possible tomorrow, isn't it?

MARK: Yes, I see that.

Let me repeat that: "An apology is not about yesterday, it's about a possible tomorrow." I believe that this is a very important concept. Yesterday is filled not only with someone's misdeeds for which an apology would seem appropriate, it is also filled with your agony and the consequences of your own bad choices as you reacted badly to their misdeeds. The apology does not ameliorate all the latter issues—which have become an integral part of your being, the way you largely see the world and your reflexive emotional reactions.

Apologies from the perpetrators of your Bad Childhood are nice, but not necessary for you to have a Good Life. In keeping with the idea offered in the beginning of this chapter, of asking those who perceive themselves as conquerors of their Bad Childhoods, I requested listeners to visit my web site (*www.drlaura.com*) and answer six questions on the concept of "closure." I received hundreds of enthusiastic answers from people who had "been there, done that."

For each question, I have listed the most important and frequently expressed answers. There is a lot to learn from those answers. The first thing you'll learn is that virtually all the participants recognized that closure was not truly about yesterday, or permanence, at all.

## Six Questions on Closure

### *Question 1*: How would you define closure?

~   "Although some people would define closure as getting an 'I'm sorry, I was wrong,' from the offending party, closure for me is defined as the decision to stop obsessing about my childhood and expecting something to happen to make everything better."

~   "Closure is being able to put something behind you. Dealing with it adequately enough that it doesn't nag you daily and/or interfere with your life."

~ "I consider closure to be moving on with one's life, living in the present rather than obsessing with the past. Closure is not amnesia, nor is it hatred of your history, nor is it revenge. Closure comes once we accept the past for what it was, accept our role in it or our lack of power in the situation, and recognize and embrace the lessons learned. When we focus on creating the current reality we desire, which will lead us into the future we want to have, we have allowed closure to take place."

~ "Closure is not a fix, but an acceptance. When you allow closure, or acceptance, you can move on without animosity. If you continue to dwell on the past, it owns you!"

**Summary:** Closure is not about putting a lid on the reality of your Bad Childhood; it's not about no longer having hurt or angry feelings, both of which are probably justified reactions; it's not about having amnesia for the horrors or disappointments of your past; it's also not about not having evildoers own up or change for the better, although that would be nice!; nor is it about never catching yourself reacting as though today were yesterday. In real life there aren't any real ends or closing. Even the death of someone hurtful to you in the past still leaves you with that history. So, what hope is there? There is tons of hope if you are flexible enough to shift your attention from yesterday to what you want to have for the rest of your life.

If anything, closure is about a commitment to a life determined by your choices and your actions, instead of a simple reaction to historical pain.

### *Question 2*: How can one obtain closure?

~    The internal strength to move on. There has to be an understanding that only healthy choices are acceptable options. There has to be the internal strength to move on, and fill whatever gap has been life with other more healthy and life affirming choices. I know I need to be a strong person every day in order to get up and live my life, given what I have been put through as a child."

~    If you love where you are in your life, it's a waste of time and energy to hate where you've been. If you go on a journey and end up rolling down a mountain, falling off a ravine, being dragged by a swift-moving stream, get dumped off a water fall, and wake up to find yourself in a beautiful valley filled with warm sun, nurturing pools, abundant fruit and adoring friends—why waste time cursing the trip that brought you to Paradise?"

~    "Ceremonially, and by strength of will. Flush that proverbial fishy down the toilet and sing taps if you have to, to give yourself a formal point of ending for that period of your life."

~    "By staying busy and not spending too much time thinking about yourself, and also by counting your blessings—when I think I have it rough, I tell myself I could have been born in Bangladesh."

~    "Closure is obtained by having an attitude of forgiveness, and focusing on the positive potential of one's future."

**Summary:** As you can see, everyone sees closure as something you do, either concretely with your life and relationships, or in your attitude, making an attitude that is forward-looking, not backward-moaning.

A Good Life takes character to live with determination, to make the right choices, and courage to embrace risk-taking and endure pain and fear.

### Question 3: What works against closure?

~ "Letting those thoughts of anger and frustration linger . . . you don't have to live it anymore!"

~ "Continuing to expose yourself to the same people, places, or situations when it is best to separate."

~ "Desire for the familiar and a fear of the unknown. Creation is hard work; it takes guts to redesign yourself and to build a new life, especially if you feel weak and unsure. Instead of focusing on your weaknesses, which feeds your insecurities, congratulate yourself for possessing the strength to survive and the willingness to make a change."

~ "Having the wrong therapist, because then all you do is have a pity party where you are too self-focused."

~ "Continuing to be inexorably drawn to keep working at changing your past, you know, if you give your mother everything she wants then maybe she'll finally love you, or if you do whatever your dad says, maybe he'll stop browbeating you. Give it up, it doesn't work."

**Summary:** Simply put, what stands between your bitter past and your better future is your attempt to swim to the other end of the swimming pool without being willing to let go of the side you're on!

### *Question 4:* **Is closure a permanent fix?**

~ "Loaded question. Nothing is permanent because life evolves; the future is built by the present and plays off the past. Odd things will happen which remind you of past emotions and former times; learn to recognize these emotions when they pop up and keep in mind that you are in control of your life now. New circumstances will create new patterns, and now that your life has changed, you do not need to expect that history will repeat itself. Remind yourself that you can control your reactions; often our reactions are what provoke the next event—new reactions will evoke a new series of events."

~ "No, you'll almost always have little reminders."

~ "For me, closure had meant that I wouldn't be upset by some defined circumstance anymore. However, when a stranger comes up to you in the mall and asks if you have spoken to a particular person, or a movie hits too close to home, it is impossible not to be shaken. Having peace in my life in general now, though, makes those encounters less traumatic."

~ "Yes, if it stops destructive behavior."

~ "Closure is not a cure, therefore it is not a permanent fix."

**Summary:** What is in your past is in your memories and guts. There will be both predictable and spontaneous moments when the past will stand up in front of you and dare you to regress into a fearful or self-loathing blob. The difference between you and blobs is your inner fortitude and the connection to those who love you; both those factors will keep you on an even keel, centered, ultimately triumphantly peaceful and resolved to enjoy life.

### *Question 5:* **What benefits come from closure?**

~    "Peace."

~    "You gain control of your life, sleep better, and love more. Being able to focus on helping others instead of always and only being lost in your own troubles."

~    "The biggest benefit was to let go of the anger I had balled up inside of me. It wasn't an overnight thing, but just the decision to stop letting it rule my life was a relief. My relationship with my parents is easy now that I'm not trying to squeeze apologies [and compensation] from them."

~    "Hopefully, the ultimate benefits are the release of negative emotion and a change to develop more positive emotions like joy, hope, and appreciation."

~    "I needed closure to live in reality. I am not a stupid woman, but when I put my blinders on and react like the little hurt girl I used to be, while in my adult world, I screw up big time."

**Summary:** The benefit of closure is that you get to actually lead a full and richer life, as opposed to being an example of arrested development.

### *Question 6:* Is closure necessary for a good life?

~   "I know it is for me! It helps me to break old patterns. Otherwise, I am caught in the loop of old habit."

~   "Living in present reality is necessary for a good life."

~   "Closure is absolutely necessary for a happy life. We all experience disappointment and pain. If we dwell on those, we can be consumed by them. If we accept that there are things over which we have no control [like our history], we can move on."

~   "Yes, because then we can focus in on helping others instead of being lost in our own troubles. This is a much more satisfying life."

~   "Actually, you can't count on closure to make a life good, you have to try to make your life good, and in doing so hope that you gain closure."

**Summary:** I like the last answer the best. When you turn to my description of resilience, you'll see that it is all about how to lead a quality life, and nothing about rectifying the past. You'll also see that having a Good Life absolutely does not require a quality childhood; it does require your grit, commitment, and action to do the things that define and create a Good Life. As your life then progresses, the strength of the impact or interference to your life of your Bad Childhood becomes naturally minimized. The behavior changes first—the emotional aspects follow the behaviors, rarely the other way around.

In conclusion, one listener wrote: *"I don't know if this is helpful, but I will tell you that I had friends that were always talking about 'getting closure' for childhoods, relationships, etc., and I thought it was something tangible that someday I could achieve. Long story short, at twenty-nine, when I was about to have my first baby, I thought to myself, 'How long does it take?!' So, I stopped waiting for it and decided to live a happy life."*

That decision, my friends, is all the so-called closure you need! I would like formally, at this point, to trade in the term closure for *resilience*. Resilience is the quality that really improves your life, not any concept of things being over and done with.

Resilience implies that you are:

- motivated to make things better
- willing to form trusting relationships
- going to identify and recognize the life situations that trigger emotional crises echoing your Bad Childhood and make efforts to control your reactions, ultimately regaining control of your feelings, instead of being a slave to them
- changing your distorted ways of looking at people and situations by giving the people in today the benefit of the doubt and by a commitment to communication

Resilience means to adapt (conform more appropriately to today's experiences and challenges) and tolerate (allow for frustrations without lashing out at life, others, or yourself) life on its current terms, rather than through the prism of yesterday's miseries and miserable people. This transformation does require something from you (vs. closure, which is something that's supposed to happen to you):

1. Developing interests (distractions, and not just living, but creating!)
2. Developing your unique gifts and talents (your existence has meaning to the world community)
3. Self-discipline (staying with your positive efforts in spite of boredom, temptations, laziness, or a surge of historical negativity)
4. Willingness to hope and dream (appreciate the blessing of life and loves)
5. Open-mindedness to new ideas (abdicating rigidity for options and possibilities)
6. Tolerance for distress (accepting the thorns with the petals)
7. Insight into your sensitivities, perceptions, and reactions (taking responsibility for your actions)
8. A shifted focus onto the well-being of others (compassion brings joy)
9. Determination of a philosophical framework for your life and work (meaning/purpose)
10. Patience with yourself, others, and life (inner peace)

You can decide to be resilient.

And remember, from this point on in this book, and your life, the word is *resilience,* not *closure.*

FOUR

# About Your Parents . . .

*Um, I'm calling today because, I actually just came from a counselor's office, and, uh, I've been having problems with—well, my whole life I've been having problems with my dad, and . . .*

**—James, a caller**

*I don't know how to feel and what to do . . . I mean, she is my mother . . .*

**—Rhonda, a caller**

### Elephants Don't Purr

A listener wrote: *"I noticed a number of your callers were complaining about their parents not being what they hoped they would be. You helped me to deal with my own disappointment with my father some years ago when you said, 'If I have a Chihuahua and I want him to be a Doberman, he will not turn into a Doberman no matter how nicely I treat him, or how much I hope it were true.'*

*"The first time I heard you say that, Dr. Laura, I felt myself let go of the pain, the anger, and the disappointment I had been harboring since childhood. Never before, or since has any one illustration impacted the quality of my life so completely. I can now have interactions with my father and come away feeling happy, because I don't go into them expecting something that I know he cannot give. I am satisfied with what I get from him because I recognize that this is all he can or will do. And, since I'm not invested in trying to get more out of him, I am relaxed and calm—and don't lay about sobbing for hours afterward. Thank you."*

Giving up "hope" that your mom or dad will ever become the loving, kind, supportive, nurturing, fun, and understanding parent of your deepest desires sounds like a downright depressing place to go, and that's understandable. Your mom and/or dad may never morph into terrific parents because they're mentally ill, evil, mean, seriously self-centered, insensitive, angry, or weak, profoundly flawed people, or dead and gone. It might even be that they're just not very bright, astute, or insightful concerning raising children and dealing with adult children. They may never have the character to admit to how they've hurt their children; they may never commit to growing and changing.

Does "giving up hope" necessarily mean that you have to give up your relationship with them? Not necessarily. However, I would recommend strongly that you do just that if they continue to be destructive or dangerous to you and your new family, if/when you have one. (More about bad parent life-extractions later on.) I make the distinction often on my program between "evil" and "annoying" parents. Evil ones are to be excised; those who are variations of annoying can be tolerated and dealt with in mature, patient, firm, consistent, sometimes limited ways. It means, though, that you have to develop the ability to accept the limitations inherent in that parent and the relationship.

The listener above who wrote about the Doberman/ Chihuahua distinction gives a perfect example of giving up hope without giving up that parent. In fact, I believe that most people dealing with difficult parents are not dealing with evil, destructive, or dangerous parents from whom they need to permanently separate. In some ways, those are the easiest situations to confront because they are black and white. It is when parents are "annoying" that they cause the most difficulty for their adult children, who resist accepting the limitations of "what is." I always remind people that we live in the land of "what is," and not the land of "what I want/wish/ need."

Most people call me with an all-or-none mentality; that is, either they continue to slog it out with a recalcitrant, difficult parent, because they refuse to accept "what is"—or all bets are off—excommunication! Since they usually feel too guilty with excommunication, after a short period of time with no contact, they revert back to slogging it out, with the consequences of ugly fights, hurt feelings, and much of their life taken up with the emotional turmoil. The resulting emotional turmoil usually results in problems at work, with children, and with spouses, and often with drug or alcohol abuse to medicate those bad feelings away.

The good news I have for you is that giving up hope is one of the healthiest, most life-affirming things you could do for yourself! That is, of course, if you follow my two-point plan: accept, and don't pout.

James called my program and we ended up dealing with just that issue.

JAMES: I've been married for seven years, we have three kids, six, three, and two. I feel like I—I can't walk away from this poor relationship with my dad. I keep trying to reestablish it and I keep getting kicked in the teeth, for lack of a better term.

James went on to tell me that he had just come back from a therapist's office, where he had gone with his wife to deal with his "father issue." His dilemma was that the therapist told him that he had to accept the kind of person his dad is, that he's not personable, and there's never going to be warm mushies. His wife had an alternative position; she wants him to walk away and stop letting his dad "kick him in the teeth."

James's wife is concerned that James will do well for about six months, and then he will call his dad and try to arrange some sort of activity with James or the whole family, and his father will cancel every time; for thirty-one years! You'd think he'd know better than to call with the same old, always rejected invitation. No, instead he sets himself up for that familiar abandonment again and then suffers and suffers—and makes his family do the same.

DR. LAURA: I think I understand the difference in their perspective. Your wife lives with you, your therapist doesn't. The problem that your wife is having with you is that you pout!

JAMES: Right.

DR. LAURA: And feel and act each time like it was the first time it's ever happened. The reason your wife's upset and wants some finality to all this is that she sees that you can't handle the truth!

JAMES: Okay.

DR. LAURA: If you would make a call every six months and

say, "Dad, come to the party on Tuesday," hang up the phone realizing he was never going to come, and then get on with your life, your wife would have no problem with you making those phone calls.

Instead, every six months, when one would imagine you'd developed some acceptance, you voluntarily throw yourself back into the predictable pit of emotional hell.

JAMES: Definitely.

DR. LAURA: You should be in therapy, but for the sole purpose of learning how not to hurt your family when you're voluntarily reliving your lifelong disappointment, again and again.

JAMES: That's a good point.

DR. LAURA: Because what your father's done in the past to you, hurt your feelings, you are now doing to your family with all your suffering. So you have to be the one to stop. You can't imagine asking somebody else to change when you're not willing.

JAMES: Good point.

James just keeps fighting "what is," continuing to test the "what is" to see if it has changed yet. What he's looking for is the romantic notion of a loving bond between himself and his dad. It is almost as if he can't appreciate himself and his life until that fantasy is attained. So unless his father becomes an entirely new person, James is never going to allow himself to have a Good Life. His father's behaviors get to dictate James's happiness and worth?

Newsflash: no matter how hard you try to bang on a wall, it won't turn into a door. You don't have the power to make people be other than who they are. You can, however, learn to be more than you've been.

James keeps re-creating a specific scene between himself

and his dad, with James as a helpless, dependent, sad, hopeful little boy. James needs to become a man. Here's an example of what he would do as a man: I bet if he just spontaneously went to his dad's workplace and had a cup of coffee with him, with small talk about some sports team, his father would be able to handle that, and he'd have a more realistic perspective of his father.

That more realistic perspective would probably include his father's deep-seated insecurities, which make him supremely insensitive to his role in life as a father. That more realistic perspective would also include the insight that his father's behavior isn't personal; in other words, it's not about James being unlovable, it's about a father being handicapped in the ability to be loving department. The acceptance of this truth will set James free from his nightmares and uptight existence with his family.

The largest part of acceptance is not fighting history or reality, and realizing that you are now supposed to be an autonomous adult, at least somewhat insulated from specious parental assaults—both in your head and/or to your face— by the protection of your perspective, attitude, and quality of life you've built and/or intend to create. (Please read last sentence three times before moving on.)

### The Princess and the Pea

If I remember the children's story "The Princess and the Pea" correctly, the test for finding out if the sweet young lass was truly the princess was that no matter how many mattresses were piled up, the princess all the way on top could feel the pea on top of the bottommost mattress because a princess's skin is so delicate. She was the princess, so she had a bad night. If you are the hypersensitive prince or princess, your life is a perpetual bad day!

Rhonda, a caller, was just such a "princess" who asked me if she should write a letter to her mother expressing the hurt she has caused her for the majority of her life. "How do I handle situations where she is constantly putting me, my mothering skills down . . . my husband and my . . ."

DR. LAURA: Why do you go on so emotionally about what your mother says or wants?

RHONDA: I guess after so many years of hearing every negative thing that can possibly come out of her mouth from what type of washer and dryer I buy, it just gets a little bit mind-boggling.

DR. LAURA: First of all, you have got to become a little less sensitive. Somebody has to be able to make a comment about a washer-dryer without you going into hysterics. Rhonda, you've got to be stronger, and you have to be less sensitive to the things that really don't matter or you're going to have trouble your whole life with strong-willed-type people.

RHONDA: You're right. But she was telling me I was financing it wrong—she thought I should go get a line of credit instead of buying them outright.

DR. LAURA: And for *that* or things like that you call about writing her a letter hitting her with the hurt she has caused you for the majority of your life? That really doesn't sound equivalent at all; that's a cannon against a peashooter. You have to learn to differentiate between what is mean and what is just her aggressively and compulsively giving her opinion. You are taking each and everything she says as a stab.

While my explanation to Rhonda sounds rational, reasonable, and correct, what makes it difficult for her, and most adults, to get past feeling like the disapproved-of little child? The answer is a determination to not see beyond their own pain, into the reality of who their parent is.

I went on to explain that to Rhonda, but I bet that you will see some of your personal situation in this answer:

DR. LAURA: Your mother is very insecure; consequently she needs to be needed and she needs to be important. That is why she has opinions about everything. You are a very insecure person, and you need constant validation and approval to feel good about yourself. Can those two people exist in the same place at the same time? No!

And that is what is going on between you and your mother. You don't realize, I think, how extremely insecure she is and that she has little awareness of how to love you as a mother. She has no clue. She is too afraid. She knows that she is not lovable, so she tries to be a Mrs. Know-it-all to compensate. That's her gift. It isn't love. But that is her version of caring about you.

The first thing I believe that you need to do is to see how fragile that big-mouthed woman you can't stand really is, because I think now that when she opens her mouth and starts giving an opinion, you will realize that she doesn't know what else to do to connect.

If she heard me saying this to you right now, half of her would cry, and the other half would get angry. The half that would cry is the part that knows the truth is being spoken. The part of her that would get angry is the self-protective part that doesn't know how to be healthy. So she defends herself, and when she defends against the awareness that she may not be motherly, she gets aggressive.

Now, to you. Even though you can't stand her guts, because you think she is making you feel bad or stupid, you are so desperate to have her love—and this is the place I want you to move away from. She is not equipped to ever give you what you need and want, and what any child reasonably needs and wants. Consequently, since you don't know she is not able, you're doubling your efforts to stay connected, try to make it work, and getting emotionally upset because you're not accepting her for who she is.

So, if you would stand back—and I'm not saying this is easy—look at her as damaged goods, realize that what she does is out of her fear and inadequacy, and not take it so personally! Since you've made yourself so dependent upon her validation, when she argues with you, even about the frying pan you've bought, you're basically so insecure from how crappy a mother she's been that you second-guess yourself, and that's why you get so upset. You've got too much emotion invested in your mommy loving you if she approves and agrees with your decisions and choices. Your logic has been that "My mother is not approving of what I've done, so she doesn't love me, so I'm upset."

Rhonda, your children adore you, even when they're being annoying; your husband adores you, although he probably wishes you'd get intimate with him more; your friends adore you, even when they're tired of hearing you weep about your mother. There are times that you simply have to look around the world and realize that when you're an adult, the validation, approval, and love *are* coming from many places—you don't have to just rely on your mother.

It is what we call neurotic for you to keep trying to squeeze a rock to get fruit juice out of it. You repeat it—it doesn't work. You keep doing it, it still doesn't work. That's your life up to now, Rhonda. What you have to do is stand back and say, "She's a rock, and I'm not going to be able to get fruit juice out of her, but I am getting it out of my kids, my friends, my cousin, my dear husband."

RHONDA: I feel like you know me. This is really strange. I mean, you're talking to me and I feel like you have just stepped into my family for the last twenty years!

DR. LAURA: I just want to help you enjoy your life.

RHONDA: You have, and I'm going to really take it to heart. My husband is recording this so I can listen to it again.

DR. LAURA: That's wonderful.

Probably the biggest step in going from a Bad Childhood to a Good Life is being able to see your parents as separate people who have good and bad aspects—in varying proportions, of course, and not just as extensions of you. Infants don't understand that it's Mommy's breast that is feeding them; they see the breast as an extension of themselves. Healthy psychological development, which is obviously helped along by "nondysfunctional" families, is supposed to result in you being an autonomous adult, bonded to your parents, but no longer totally dependent upon them for your next emotional breath.

*"You're so vain, I bet you think my life is about you . . ."*

With apologies to Carly Simon, I would like you to imagine that your errant, difficult, or woefully inadequate parents is singing this to you. How enraging! It's natural for you to be angry at your parents for seeming to brush aside their painful, complicated impact on you. After all, you were an innocent child whose development depended on their sensitivity to your unique qualities and their willingness to fulfill basic emotional, psychological, and physical requirements of any child; they let you down and you have to pay the price. True enough.

Now that you're an adult, let's move to the next level. Chris, a caller, is a young man who called me complaining that he just recently met his biological father for the first time face-to-face.

CHRIS: He told me that there is a thousand something minutes in a day, and that he didn't have one for me, and hum, it really hurt me a lot because I understand that when I was younger he had to adopt me out because he had problems. But he just went and adopted two other children, but he wants nothing to do with me—his only biological child, his only son. I feel like he must have a lot of anger toward me and I don't understand why.

DR. LAURA: You think he is rejecting "Chris"?

CHRIS: Yes.

DR. LAURA: Well, that means he really knew and knows who you are, and he's made a judgment that who you are is icky, therefore, he doesn't want to have you in his life. Is that what you're saying?

CHRIS (sound of exasperation): Uh . . . I don't know.

DR. LAURA: I need a "yes" or a "no," please.

CHRIS: Yes.

DR. LAURA: How could he make a judgment about you personally—to reject you—when he doesn't even know you?

CHRIS: I don't understand the reason why somebody would

do that. I'd love my child and I could never do something like that.

DR. LAURA: Ah, because you don't understand the why of what would motivate a man like him, you rush to fill the vacuum with the explanation that it must mean something bad about you? That's a dangerous place to go because you end up undermining your own lifelong happiness because of a false assumption.

You don't know that there are men who put explosives around their children's bodies and send them out to explode, killing themselves and innocent people?

CHRIS: Yes.

DR. LAURA: Right. How do you understand them? Would you do that to your kid? Is it because the kid is unlovable?

CHRIS: No.

DR. LAURA: That's correct. So you're aware that there are people, that there are men who don't love their children? Are you aware that there are some men who can't love, who can't face responsibilities, who are unbelievably self-centered, who rob, cheat, or murder?

CHRIS: Yes.

DR. LAURA: Okay, so you are aware that there are some bad men out there.

CHRIS: Yes.

DR. LAURA: Well, one of them is your bio-dad. It's not personal.

CHRIS: Okay, so that's just the way *he* is.

DR. LAURA: That's correct.

CHRIS: He's just a loser.

DR. LAURA: That's correct. And when he looked into your face, what he saw was his bad self for abandoning you and he slapped you back. And that's how we know he is still a loser and a bad guy—he's not making it up to you. So, you cannot take it personally. Your mom made a booboo and "did it" with the wrong guy.

CHRIS: Yes. You've made me feel so much better, Dr. Laura. Thank you *so* much.

Let's be honest here: not having your mommy or daddy in your life is a painful loss, the hurt from which is unavoidable. There should be no question about that in your mind. However, blaming or punishing yourself for your mommy or daddy's choices in life is an *avoidable* hurt. Don't forget, the reason they are your bio-parents is because they simply are two human beings who had sex—and that wasn't about you, either!

## The Second Coming

What happens when an abandoning parent attempts to re-connect and become part of your life again? I'll tell you what happens: confusion! Part of you wants what you never had, the other part of you is ferociously angry, so you go back and forth in your thinking and don't quite know what to do to handle that parent, or your feelings.

Travis, a twenty-two-year-old man, called my program with just that problem. He had not seen nor heard from his mother in fifteen years. He called telling me that he wasn't sure how to handle her out-of-the-blue phone call, where she told him she wanted to know what he was doing and encouraged him to have a relationship with her.

TRAVIS: I'm so confused. I guess I just want so badly to have a relationship with her. But, she just destroyed my dad. She destroyed me and my brother.

There it is: in one breath you can hear the longing and the anger. I told him that she had indeed not destroyed his dad. His dad's been working and raising the boys. I reminded him that she hasn't destroyed him, either, since he is a well-mannered, intelligent, competent young man.

DR. LAURA: You are not destroyed. Don't give her that much credit! And that's like saying your dad, and all the other friends and family who helped, had little impact—that the only or prevailing impact is from the person who *wasn't* there. She hasn't destroyed your life. She robbed you of a mommy. But she hasn't destroyed your life—only you can do that.

Travis, do you know how your dad would feel if he'd heard you say that just now? He would say, "What am I, chopped liver?" How would you feel?

TRAVIS: I'd probably feel not too good.

DR. LAURA: Right! You have to get a balanced view here, Travis. A lot of people stayed and loved you and took care of you, isn't that so?

TRAVIS: That's true.

DR. LAURA: I suggest you meet her at some coffee shop and sit down and tell her how you feel about her abandonment. Let her know also that any of her excuses are not interesting, and that accountability would be more convincing of her desire to develop something with you.

TRAVIS: Yeah, I'd like to hear what she has to say.

I think it's healthy of Travis to meet with his bio-mom ("mother" is a title given to the person who does the job of raising, not just giving birth—although we are all grateful for that!). Remember, though, that a meeting is not a relationship. A mother–son relationship and bond never developed and can't be promised or demanded now. However, it is possible for them to become friends, as long as she takes full responsibility for her actions and has changed.

A meeting or a conversation with a bio-parent you've had little or nothing to do with your whole life gives you the opportunity to ask questions. I never felt that "venting" with yelling, recriminations, and ferocious tears was useful. I believe you should see this as a fact-finding mission, one in which you learn about them, not about yourself—you've already been there for all of your development!

A woman in her forties called with the same dilemma, but with no confusion. She knew she didn't want her mother, who had abandoned the family by joining a convent, in her life. The problem she was calling me with was that just about everybody was telling her that she was obligated to have her mother in her life. She told me she was feeling incredibly pressured and torn even though she was sure she wanted nothing of her mother.

I suggested to her that the weakness she felt in the face of that pressure was actually her own ambivalence. Ambivalence means you have some feelings of wanting and other feelings of not wanting to be connected to your bio-mom (or dad). Those two urges are in you at the same time. The pressure is really from within you. Nobody can pressure you if there isn't a core part of you that "wants," badly.

PAT: Well, I want to because—she was my mother.
DR. LAURA: Yes, "was." And then she abdicated her job.
PAT: Right.
DR. LAURA: So, if she is back in your life—that can take a number of forms. But you have to reconcile how angry

you are and how you want to hurt her. You've learned to survive without her, and you're not willing to be vulnerable to her. You have to reconcile your longing with your fears and anger. I think the best way to do that is to sit with her and say, "I don't care how you justified this in terms of your commitment to God and to Church, but you abandoned your children, and I don't easily forgive you for that. I've learned to survive without a mother, and I'm perfectly capable of doing that for the rest of my life. So, while you gave birth to me and raised me for a while, and then abandoned all your children, you're no mother in the classical sense of a loving mother. So, I don't know what or if our relationship is going to be—but don't push for things you haven't earned, and we'll see how this goes."

PAT: That's really nice! But what about the people who pressure me and tell me it's the Christian thing to do?

DR. LAURA: Recognize that's their opinion, and that you, as I said before, are using that pressure to get yourself past your anger to satisfy your need. When they start talking that line, say, "Stop, I've heard it before. Thank you for your opinion." I'm telling you, sit with this woman and tell her she is not at this point your "mother." She abandoned her children and rationalized it as a godly thing to do. Frankly, I see this as a bit blasphemous: doing something horrendous to your children and your vows in the name of God. If she is unwilling to deal with the truth, be done with it and her.

PAT: Okay.

You'll notice that I do not recommend blaming-style, angry, sobbing confrontations. I don't believe they are at all constructive. That's the old "closure" style of thinking: a big blow-up will clear the air and all is well. Nope. This is the new "resilience" style of thinking: you set out the truth of their actions and set the parameters for any possible future. You then present yourself as you largely are or are working toward becoming: a competent, centered, autonomous person who will love and accept love from the significant persons in your life— in spite of not having the greatest head start.

## You Shall Overcome

Whenever I discuss issues of forgiveness on my radio program, I am deluged with scriptural arguments about this apparently sensitive subject. I do not intend to argue these points here. I am concerned whenever seriously wronged and damaged people call me, now feeling doubly bad about themselves because they are getting pressured, out of religious obligation, to forgive those who hurt them. One of the most odious of these situations is a family in which the father/stepfather has molested one or more of the children, and later the children, as adults, are pressured to "forgive and forget" and to go on as though everything is "all better." They are encouraged to be physically affectionate with the abuser, and to leave their children in his charge because "we are family."

It is obvious that most of that pressure to forgive is about someone's avoidance of legal consequences, public embarrassment, or any change in marital/family circumstances. The children, abused once, are now abused again by the denial.

It is also typical that the perpetrator may indeed "apologize"; however, when the wrongdoer has not taken true responsibility and embraced the consequences of their behaviors, nor have they made some sort of appropriate restitution, nor do they seem particularly remorseful, nor have they made concrete efforts to not repeat their actions (all these qualities are aspects of repentance), then making the hurt party accept this insincere apology is just another form of abuse.

There are religious traditions that prescribe forgiveness of all enemies and offenders in an unqualified way, in other words, without the repentance of the wrongdoer, as a way of demonstrating their faith in and love for God. There are other traditions that require confession to church authorities as a precursor to asking for forgiveness. I will leave your particular religious sensibilities to you. But I will say that I believe that many people do not really understand their own scriptures and "dumb down" important concepts like forgiveness into a knee-jerk whitewash, demanding premature forgiveness from themselves or others, only to cause more damage.

I am approaching this from a more universal spiritual and psychotherapeutic perspective: I believe in the definition of forgiveness that involves you renouncing anger or resentment against that person, but does not excuse or pardon them for their harmful actions, nor does it require you to stay involved with them in any concrete way.

I believe that forgiveness does not require forgetting the wrongs against you (or others); it should not absolve them from their guilt, nor from the appropriate consequences, but it does require you to move beyond certain emotions like humiliation, grief, resentment, rage, and so forth.

Your forgiveness is not for their sake, it is for yours—it becomes a commitment to your own well-being. You cannot have a good life if your mind and heart are dominated by negative emotions.

Jane, a listener, came to a healthy place about forgiving her father: *"Hi, I wanted to tell you that I have begun to pray for my dad and that has helped me tremendously. For years I seethed and cried and refused to accept what was. I just wanted that apology that has never come (and may never). This holding of the pain close to your heart hurts only yourself. When I gave up hope that I could do anything and gave it over to God and began to pray—I felt a lot of peace. I don't feel angry with my dad anymore. Praying brings me compassion and understanding that we are all flawed and hopefully will exit this world triumphant and strong, not as twisted and wretched souls. I now want the best for him, and if this is the bad path he continues to go down, I hope that he can find peace from the demons that torment his soul in the end. I think I feel sorry for him—yet, I continue to protect myself from him."*

I believe that Jane is approaching forgiveness in a healthy way.

Most of you have gone through some, if not all, of the basic phases in growing from a Bad Childhood to the forgiveness that stimulates a Good Life:

1. Shock and denial
2. Awareness and recognition that you have been abused, hurt, and offended
3. Appropriate expression of feelings of hurt, grief, and anger
4. Validation of your perspective; some form of justice
5. A plan for minimizing opportunity to be hurt by the wrongdoer again
6. Letting go and moving on with your life

Demanding forgiveness by yourself or from another before numbers 1 through 5 are experienced will likely just

keep you stuck in the bad feelings, now more helpless than
ever to have a Good Life.

Forgiveness is about, as Judy wrote, *". . . releasing myself
from the bondage of hating them for what they did to me. That the
hate would only destroy me . . . I know that it is the best thing for
me."*

She's right.

How do you "Honor Thy Father and Thy Mother" when
your parents are the bad guys?

Dealing with evil or awful parents is probably the singular
most difficult issue of this commandment. Some religious
authorities hold that a child is not bound to honor a wicked
parent as long as that parent does not repent.* Still, that child
is forbidden to intentionally cause that parent grief. It is possible to maintain minimal, polite contact, assist a bad parent
with such basic needs as food or housing and medicine, or
even help them as they're dying. It may not be ideal, and it
may not salve your feelings, but that small something you do
ennobles your soul.

You may have wondered if blowing the whistle on a
parent's horrible behavior is dishonoring your parent by "causing them grief." No, it's not. Causing an unrepentant parent to
accept the consequences of their actions, with, for example,
legal consequences, informing relevant parties of their potential danger from the hands of that parent, taking steps to make
sure you are not victimized, or admonishing that parent in private to avoid humiliation are all attempts to get them back on
the right track. All attempts to get your parent on the correct

---

*As I elaborated on in my book *The Ten Commandments: The Signifi-
cance of God's Laws in Everyday Life.*

moral track are forms of honoring them. Avoiding, ignoring, excusing, hiding from, or denying the dangerous or destructive behaviors (even drug or alcohol abuse) is not honoring that parent because your behaviors do not in the long run influence that parent to get back on a moral track; whether you fail or not is not the important issue!

Another listener wrote of her concerns with "honoring your father and your mother." Her mother had been so ferociously physically violent with her that a great deal of her childhood was spent recovering from broken feet and arms. Saying that she, the child, was evil, her mother would lock her up in a chest or closet for hours or over a day. She was made permanently blind by her mother's punch in the eye. As though this were not enough, her father sexually molested her.

Her father has been deceased for five years; her mother is still alive and lives several hours away from her. Last summer, her mother came to her home with a knife after hiring a private investigator to track her down.

*"It pained me to have to call the police and have my mother arrested for this incident. The Bible doesn't say, "Honor your mother and your rather if they deserve it." As a Christian I grappled with many ideas of what this commandment could mean. Surely it didn't mean that I should pretend that nothing happened and try to have a normal relationship with my mother. God never calls us to be stupid!*

*"Honoring my mother means that I shouldn't give her the chance to sin against me. If she threatens me, I have to lovingly tell her that what she is choosing is unacceptable and that I will not allow it to happen. Honoring my mother means giving her boundaries with respect to my life. Though she tries to control me, I don't have to give in to her inappropriate requests to move back home, to send her money, or other such requests.*

*"Honoring my mother means that I have to give credit to her for the good things that she did for me such as placing me in good schools, and helping to pay for my college education.*

*"Honoring my mother means not throwing her deficits in her face.*

*"Honoring my mother means that I have to make an effort to have a relationship with her in a safe way. When my mom is taking her medication (diagnosed as schizophrenic and bipolar) she can be a nice person. Honoring my mother means having dinner with her when she's on her medication and telling her honestly that I can't safely spend time with her when she's refusing to take her medication.*

*"Listening to your program, Dr. Laura, has taught me that my mother will never be my mother; she will never tell me that she loves me or is proud of me. Honoring my mother means realizing that she can't be the mother I would have wanted and needed. I can't require her to be the mother I need, so I have many, many women in my life who give me the motherly love, affection, encouragement, advice, and compassion that my own mother was and is unable to give."*

These insights are remarkable enough—but you should know that the writer still fears the dark and enclosed spaces, will always be blind in one eye, is not able to have children, and won't be able to walk for much longer because of the many times her feet were broken.

*"I am alive, Dr. Laura, in spite of the reality that I should have died many times over. I am a teacher of some wonderful students and have so many loved ones in my area that are so very supportive and loving toward me. God has been good to me, and I am thankful."*

Quite honestly, of all the wonderful letters I have included in this book, this one touched and humbled me the most. It is so inspiring to see someone so physically and emotionally devastated still grateful for life, God, her friends, and the opportunity to do good works. She is even grateful to what she gleans as the positives of her mother. What incredible depth—what an incredible role model!

It is important to note that the commandment is to "honor," not "love," your father and mother. You cannot make yourself love even a parent, or force yourself to feel a bond that was never developed.

Another listener wrote that she has chosen to accept that her mother was and is incapable of mothering. *"I 'honor' my mother the best I can by making sure that her basic care needs are met. I do get some satisfaction out of knowing that I am 'doing the right thing.' And she has helped me in one surprising way—given how painful her lack of mothering was for me, I made a complete and early commitment to be 'my kids' mom.' I learned my lesson well, even if it was from the 'flip-side' perspective."*

This letter was written by a woman whose mother was the town drunken slut (primarily with other women's husbands), threw constant hysterical or anger fits, blamed her daughter for ruining her life, feigned multiple suicide attempts and blamed that on her daughter, and finally put a gun to her daughter's head demanding love. Basically she was completely self-absorbed, totally incompetent as a parent, unpredictable, and dangerous.

Now, for the most part in this book, I have not routinely described the specifics of the caller or writer's Bad Childhood; that is because this is not meant to be a voyeuristic tome and the issues are the same regardless of the details of your Bad Childhood. However, in these two cases I found it important for you to see the unbelievable depth of depravity that a person can face and still find joy in life, beauty in love, and compassion for the source of their decidedly Bad Childhood.

The latter writer also wrote that with the help of a good therapist and a wonderful husband and kids, she has decided not to let those experiences cripple her or define who she is. She attributes her healing to the strength and courage God has given her to take care of her mother's basic human necessities during her failing years, financially and with "duty" visits. She doesn't invest too much emotionally in any dialogue with her mother, who is still so self-focused she doesn't even realize the difference.

These are two examples of resilience and a refusal to lose humanity.

### Finding the Oreo Cookie in the Compost Heap

One of the most significant mind-sets for a Good Life is positive thinking. When callers want to complain on and on about their parents, friends, or spouses, I usually ask them to give me five to ten really important, wonderful, good things about that person as the price for me hearing the bad stuff. This assignment is largely about helping the caller calm down and get perspective, and teaching them not to dismiss the valuable aspects that would buoy them in their lives and relationships.

A great example of this came from a listener, Kris, whose mother died as an alcoholic in denial. Kris never shed a tear about his mother's passing, nor did he feel any loss about her death. In fact, it scared him a bit that he felt nothing whatsoever in terms of grief or sadness. When his mother died, he mostly was relieved that his suffering at the hands of his mother was over. As the oldest child, while his siblings were finishing college and starting their own families, he provided for her necessities since she had squandered her own money away.

"*So,*" Kris wrote, "*I was all set to tell you why I could not honor my mother because of her alcoholism and the detriment that caused to our family. But, I can't! I really have a lot to thank her for, though I know the adult I became was not because of any grand parenting plan on her part.*

"*When she was too drunk to:*

- *wash the clothes, I learned to run a washer and dryer*
- *fix the meals, I became a fairly decent cook*
- *take care of my baby sister, I learned how to change diapers, make formula, and how to entertain a two-year-old*
- *pay the bills, I learned how to live within my means*
- *help me with my homework, I figured it out myself*
- *to pay for my college education, I did it myself*
- *run to my aid when I got arrested for drag racing, I suffered the consequences of my actions myself*
- *give me advice about life, love and the pursuit of happiness, I learned how to achieve the American dream on my own*

"*So, even though my mother thwarted and frustrated me for almost my entire life, I still have to give her credit for helping me become the man I am. I can't say that I loved her, but in a way I must give her some honor for the gifts she inadvertently gave me.*"

I believe Kris's analysis is something you can learn from because even negative examples are examples—of what not to do! A bad history is not destiny. You have choices in perspective, attitude, and actions. These are the stuff resilience, and therefore a Good Life, are made of.

FIVE

# How Do I Deal with My Anger, My Resentment, and My Own Crazy Self?

*I never realized that I had been cheated out of my childhood, and that I actually had a right to be angry. When I finally realized that, I did become VERY angry! Once I admitted the true feelings that I had, I could deal with them. I found that it is impossible to deal with feelings that you refuse to admit that you have.*

**—Tracy, a listener**

*It is important to people like us, who have suffered emotional abuse and mistreatment, whether it is done with or without malice and forethought, that someone like you, Dr. Laura, can recognize it is still valid abuse.*

**—Allyson, a listener**

So many callers to my program know two things:

1. That they had/are having unfortunate bio-family experiences and dynamics, and

2. That they had/are having uncomfortable interpersonal experiences and dynamics, but they're missing an understanding that numbers 1 and 2 are connected.

A perfect example of this phenomenon is a two-part call I had with Karen, a twenty-year-old woman from a divorced home, who has been with a boyfriend for about six months. Based upon her conversations with others her age, she believes they have a unique relationship—they're not sexually active because they are both serious Christians and very much into their faith, choosing to live by those moral standards.

She expressed that although they both realize it is a bit early, lately they have been discussing marriage. She offered that she's pretty serious about him, but getting physically sick with nervousness over the idea of marriage.

KAREN: It's hard for me to tell him that I love him right now. It's like, I feel horrible. I know, I know that I have issues there . . . I know that.

DR LAURA: And what do you think the issues are?

KAREN: I think I'm scared because my parents are saying, "You need to not take this so seriously."

DR. LAURA: That's the problem; they didn't take their vows seriously.

KAREN: Exactly, and that's what I told them. I said, "Okay, this is a decision that is going to affect the rest of my life, my children . . . and I can't do something, you know . . ."

DR. LAURA: Like your folks put you through.

KAREN: Exactly, and they're just well, "You can never know, you can't control divorce."

DR. LAURA: Sure you can.

Karen went on to extol the virtues of her boyfriend and her love for him, simultaneous with her pain that she felt alone because even though he's "an angel, and treats me so well, with such love and compassion," she's trying to get away from him.

KAREN (crying): I hate doing this. I'm sorry (for the crying).

I told her not to apologize for being in pain because of her parents' attitude and actions. It's not just that they were divorced, although that has its own challenges and losses, it is that they're so flip about it—suggesting that her attempts to make sure it's going to be forever are kind of wasted because "poop happens," as though they were not responsible for their own breakup.

DR. LAURA: Karen, let's pretend you were walking in the forest and a bear attacked you viciously: bit, scratched, and slammed you around a lot. Now, ten years later you are in the forest again and a beautiful doe appears. Are you going to run screaming out of the forest?

KAREN: No . . .

DR. LAURA: Why not?

KAREN: Because it is not something that is going to hurt me.

DR. LAURA: But, how do you know? An animal hurt you and this is an animal—so, it could hurt you!

KAREN: Because it doesn't have the characteristics of a bear.

I went on to ask Karen if her boyfriend has any characteristics of the "bear," in other words, her mother or father. She said, "No." I continued by asking her if she has any characteristics of either one of her parents. She said, "Yes."

DR. LAURA: Which ones?

KAREN: I'm not a very thankful person, I grow discontent very fast with things, I'm in competition always with other females, and always trying to get attention from guys, and let's see, what else? . . . I'm very dominant, which I know is going to hurt things horribly. I'm very, very controlling. And I don't give of myself easily.

Let me list Karen's self-analysis points for deeper analysis:

1. Not grateful/thankful
2. Bores easily
3. Competes with other girls/women
4. Solicits male attention
5. Dominant and controlling
6. Doesn't give of herself easily

First, I congratulated Karen for being so self-aware and for her willingness to express the shortcomings that she knows would hurt the person she loves. That automatically put her well ahead of her parents. Instead of being aware of their own individual shortcomings, acknowledging them, and doing something about them, they just split up the family. Even today, they are rationalizing that "poop happens," instead of taking responsibility for where they let each other, themselves, and their children down.

Her parents not only divorced, but went on to try again. Karen's mom got married and divorced another time and had Karen's half-brother. Her father got remarried, and is raising his new wife's daughters.

DR. LAURA: Okay, let's start with number 6—"You don't give of yourself easily." Of course not! You're afraid of being drained of the world that you put yourself into to survive—that somebody would take it and then walk away.

KAREN: Right.

DR. LAURA: Not only did your parents walk away from each other, but they walked away from you. In a child's mind, parents remarrying and either having kids or taking care of their new spouse's children, is to jump to numbers 3 and 4, which are basically the same thing: to be in competition with other kids for your own parent, and to be in competition with the new spouse for your own parent. So you were put in the position very early in your life to have to compete with adults and children for your own parents' attention!

KAREN: Okay, that makes sense.

DR. LAURA: The issue of being dominant and in control, number 5—that's just you trying to make sure that your world is going to be stable.

KAREN: Right . . . which it never was, anyway.

DR. LAURA: Now, as for number 1, "grateful." Of course you're not grateful. You're not because you're damn angry! I don't know if you have expressed your anger sufficiently to the people who ought to hear about it, and I'm not talking about beating up your parents for three years. I'm just saying that you ought to respond to your parents' flippancy about you choosing a husband by saying something like, "You know what, I'm damn angry that you had that kind of relationship, that you broke up, that you have an easy attitude about divorce, that you went and got married and made a kid and got divorced again, that you went and took care of somebody else's kid instead of me . . . frankly, I'm damn angry because . . . I was what was left at the bottom of all of that."

I think it's hard for you, Karen, to be grateful for what you do have because you are still mad at what you should have gotten and didn't.

KAREN: Right, so I feel . . . like I deserve things.

DR. LAURA: When you were a child you deserved the protection, attention, stability, direction, and love that every child needs, period. But now you're an adult, and I'm worried that you are behaving as though the rights of a child, which you largely did not get fulfilled, are yours to fulfill now, so you manipulate your boyfriend to be a better parent than you had—which no spouse can provide without abdicating his needs and rights, and continuing to contribute to your living in the past.

KAREN: Oops, guilty!

DR. LAURA: Number 2 is the only one I haven't touched upon yet, and that was the one in which you get bored and you grow discontented quickly. That's because you are afraid to hold onto anything too long—it won't stay there anyway. You grab the moment, and don't believe in longevity.

KAREN: Right.

I then told Karen that her assignment was to:

- think about the bear and doe scenario all the time, as a constant reminder to herself that she, others, and life can be quite different from what was in the past.
- let her parents know that she doesn't appreciate their negative and flimsy attitude about marriage and commitment. Hopefully, she'd get an *acknowledgment* that her anger and pains of loss are warranted; however, that's not to be a mooring ("Poor me, I'm a victim")

but a point of departure into her new journeys ("Rich me, I'm a conquerer!")

This concept of acknowledgment over apology is an important issue. I told her strongly that she needed to tell her parents her view of their actions (past and present) and the impact they've had on her. My intent is to have her present herself as a self-aware *adult*, as she faces her own fears and their defensive dismissal of those fears. Her demeanor should not be one of *poor me,* but instead of a young woman who is struggling to build something more beautiful and secure than she had in growing up.

If you are thinking that an apology from her parents is adequate or a reasonable trade-off, you're incorrect. You know how most of these apologies go: "*If* I've done anything to hurt you, sorry!" Or, "I did the best I could." Or, "It wasn't my doing, it was your mother/father." No matter how you spin it, it doesn't provide the reality check that people are entitled to when another's actions directly, intentionally or not, hurt them. In other words, her parents would do better to ignore the *apology* and give her something so much more important: an *acknowledgment* of the truth.

Want to make someone crazy? Easy! All you have to do is tell them that their perceptions are wrong and that what they experienced was in their own minds. Once people are validated in their point of view, they usually gain the strength to go forward and do the right and healthy things for a Good Life.

I received numerous commentaries from listeners who identified with Karen.

From Marion: *"Your analogy of the 'bear vs. deer in the wood' spoke to me. I keep going back to the woods, seeking out the bear and trying to get it to apologize for mauling me, but, after thirty years, that is probably not going to happen. I have to move on to a greener pasture and look for deer. And when I see a bear, I am going to play dead."*

*"I am Karen with twenty more years of experience. My parents divorced and remarried numerous times, adding half-siblings and stepsiblings along the way. I was an angry, disappointed, scared, and confused young woman. Like Karen, I'd heard a lot about the importance of commitment, but had NEVER felt the positive effects of it. The self-awareness for which you commended her will be the characteristic that will help her become the woman she wants to be. I have now been married for fifteen years and have three children who don't understand why Mommies and Daddies would ever get divorced . . . and truly, isn't that the way it should be?"*

From Patricia: *"I had never thought that my own issues (like being ungrateful, discontent, and controlling) came from my parents' divorce. Your caller's issues were some of the same issues I've been trying to overcome for the last thirty years. Wow! Your answers to her were right on. I never understood about the reason I felt that way. I only thought about how to get over it! And, you're right. I AM ANGRY. I have never liked psychology—right before my parents got divorced, my Mom started going to a class where she learned to 'worry about yourself,' and 'Make yourself happy,' without worrying about the impact on others. What kind of life is that? Thanks, you're great."*

As I've mentioned, I believe it helps tremendously to understand the connection between your childhood woes and your current outlook on life and people. Without that connection, you may be able to rationalize your pain and inappropriate behaviors by blaming others, situations, God, and anything and anyone besides your own inner turmoil, which leaves you stuck in the same place. When you recognize and acknowledge that connection, you can begin to take responsibility for your actions and defensive maneuvers, check yourself when you see yourself lapsing into old routine behaviors and patterns of feeling, and grow into a healthier and happier version of yourself.

Let's be honest here: "people pleasers," "doormats," and "martyrs" are not truly *giving* people; these are the mechanisms by which un–self-aware and emotionally challenged people attempt to manipulate others in their adult lives to feed them what they didn't get as children. Ultimately, these mind-sets are as self-centered as were the people who hurt or starved you in the first place because it is still all about *you.*

Truly giving people are comfortable with receiving and give of their deepest selves—which is the most profound form of giving there is.

## I Don't Love My Momma

Chapter Four deals indepth with the problems you may have dealing with your destructive parents. Right now I intend to explore with you how not loving a parent impacts you and what you can do to help yourself with the feelings of self-loathing and self-doubt that come along for that ugly ride.

Quite a few of you are feeling tremendous guilt because you don't feel warm, loving feelings for your mother and/or your father. One such listener wrote, *"I was born to an illegitimate parent whose life was one long succession of wrong decisions. Not just bad decisions—wrong decisions. I learned early on, against the advice and reminders of family, that I didn't really have a mother. I heard, 'She's your mother! You have to love her.'*

*"I lived with the guilt of not loving my selfish, self-centered mother. I thought there was something wrong with me. Why was I so unlovable? Why could I not please her? How I wish there had been one voice encouraging me, letting me know that the fault did not lie with me. She cared more about being somebody's shack-up honey than about being my mother.*

*"You, Dr. Laura, have been such a voice of re-affirmation for the decisions I was forced into. When I turned eighteen, I broke away and never went back. It was the best decision I ever made. I married a good man and raised three great children."*

Right now is the moment to bring to your attention that even the commandment reads "to honor" and not "to love" your father and your mother. The commandment reminds you that you have some specific obligations, but it does not require that they come from a sentiment of love. You can't be commanded to love, nor can you force yourself to.

Belinda, a caller, is torn between her lack of love or caring for her alcoholic mother who is now dying of stomach cancer, and her sense of obligation. These confusions generally peak when a parent is elderly or dying.

BELINDA: I've had a lot of issues with forgiveness toward her. I was raised in a very abusive family.

DR. LAURA: Belinda, you are under no obligation to forgive somebody who has never repented—but you are under an obligation to your own self to let certain things "go" so you can get on with your life. And there is a difference between letting things go and forgiveness. Forgiveness is a two-party exercise: repentance means that they take responsibility, have remorse, try to repair it, and not repeat it. When they don't do that, you are under no obligation to forgive, but you can decide that it is unhealthy for you to keep harboring ill feelings and just get on with your life as a healthy, happy individual dealing with current realities out of the shadows of your past.

BELINDA: Yeah. I had to decide that I wasn't going to be a victim of hers anymore. So I made a lot of changes over the past year and a half because I was in and out of the mental hospitals a lot.

DR. LAURA: Well, good. You have a lot of strength.

BELINDA: Yeah. And I just started college. But I want, when she goes, I want to feel perfectly fine with myself. That I don't have any regrets.

As Bette Davis's character said as she stood on the staircase in the film *All About Eve*, "Fasten your seatbelts, it's going to be a bumpy night." You'll probably need to brace yourself for some of what is to come because it's not politically correct in psych circles. I told Belinda that her expectation to have equanimity when her mother dies, where she'll have no regret or guilt, happens only in fairy-tale land, and she shouldn't even ask that of herself. The truth is, when a bad parent dies, whether or not you're "nice" at the end or give them dispensation for their bad acts, you're still stuck with what's evolved in you from your Bad Childhood, and not from their deathbed.

Nonetheless, I have advised many people to go to their usually estranged parent's deathbed out of pure human compassion and common decency. I do remind them, however, not to expect some magical moment. Mostly people call me back and tell me they felt pity for a person who has a parent who dies without the love of their children. I think that is a healthy—sad, but healthy—response.

Here comes another bump:

DR. LAURA: You are probably going to feel a resurgence of anger, hurt, and sadness that you really didn't have a mother. Better she hadn't existed than she torture you like she did. You know, Belinda, you're going to go through some bad emotions—and then you'll let it go again.

BELINDA: Yeah. I love her, too, whether she was abusive to me or not.

DR. LAURA: I can't buy that. I don't believe we love abusive, ugly parents.

BELINDA: I didn't love the abuse, but I love her because she was my mother.

DR. LAURA: I don't buy that. I'm sorry, I don't even like hearing that because it trivializes love. I could be the worst scum of the earth, but because I am genetically related I'm going to say that I have love? Love has to have more depth and breadth and meaning than that. I'd buy it if you told me you wish you had a mother you could love. I'd buy it if you told me you pity her, because she is a pathetic creature nobody loves. I could buy, I'm trying to learn how to love at all because I came from this. These things make sense to me. But saying you love somebody just because of a genetic relationship, I never buy that.

And I think it is something that folks who have been very damaged try to say so they have the world "love" in their lives. But you can love a lot of other people who are wonderful and healthy who aren't related at all by genetics. Save your love for them.

BELINDA: I agree with what you are saying.

DR. LAURA: Don't waste it on that woman.

BELINDA: That's exactly what I've done.

DR. LAURA: And don't think you have to say you love her in order to be a nice person.

BELINDA: Yeah, I suppose that is what I was doing. I don't want her to die feeling like I hated her all my life.

DR. LAURA: Well, she is either going to die with that thought, which was earned by her because that's the life she's led, or not give a damn.

At this point in the conversation we switched gears back to Belinda's emotional difficulties. She expressed concern that if she didn't get into all mush mode that she'd slip back into ferocious anger and be hospitalized again. I told her that having appropriate feelings, even ugly ones like anger or hate, does not mean that she's going crazy again. The craziness comes from the handling of those emotions, not their existence. We also got into the main point: with her mother's death she is going to always mourn the fact that she didn't ever have a mother. Once Mom's gone, it's final—no hope for anything to ever be different.

BELINDA: Yeah, I'd rather she just be gone than have her say some more bad things, or have that constant hope every day of my life that she is going to be somebody different, you know? I just feel that it makes it so much harder with her being alive, because in a way, she is dead already.

DR. LAURA: I am so glad you allowed yourself to say what you just said. It's healthier for you to face the truth rather than tear yourself up with what you hope for that is hopeless, blame yourself when you're blameless, and try to feel love in a loveless reality. Belinda, I think you're going to be okay.

BELINDA: I think so, too. Thank you.

Sometime after that call, Belinda wrote to me about the impact of our conversation on her. I was quite moved—and quite shocked!

Belinda is the oldest of four children, all of whom have different fathers. Her mother was obviously promiscuous, and also abused drugs and alcohol. When Belinda was eight, an upstairs neighbor and friend of her mother's sexually abused her. When she told her mother, Mom said, "Well, honey, I was abused, too, and sometimes things like that just happen." Of course, Belinda was crushed because her mother seemed to not care.

Belinda went into periods of depression and developed a victim mentality. "As far as I was concerned, all of my problems were everyone else's fault. I had been hurt and traumatized, and I deserved to be in self-pity." After numerous suicide attempts and more than fifty-six hospitalizations in one year, she began a new journey of being empowered.

She wrote: *"I wanted to let you know that I appreciate what you said to me about forgiveness and love. I have always had it in the back of my head that love is a two-way street, yet have felt guilty for not truly loving my mother. My mother is a person who is very manipulative with all of her children, putting her needs first and neglecting us.*

*"I feel relieved that I don't have to excuse my mother's actions and tell her that I forgive her or love her. I also realized one other thing from our short talk. I don't have to listen to my mother's statement that she drilled into my head: I don't have to be grateful to her because she didn't abort me. It wasn't my fault that she had me so young. I agree, love means so much more than what she gave me.*

*"I know she is my mom, I have her genes, her eyes, but not her love. I wanted to love her, but never did. I feel good that I am not her. I take life and love seriously because so much of it was spent being abused by others and myself. Dr. Laura, I agree with you—I*

*am going to be OK. Thank you for being a part of that."*

Cheryl, another listener who was also a caller, wrote to me of her reaction to our conversation. Her mother, an alcoholic throughout Cheryl's life, had three kids with three different men and was physically abusive to the point that Cheryl and her two siblings ended up in seven different foster homes before the age of nine! Mom then landed herself in prison for driving drunk and crippling a person for life.

*"You, Dr. Laura, in one phone call, took all the guilt I have been carrying away and freed me from the prison I allowed her to create around me. Years of hearing I owed her because she had one foot over her grave when she gave birth to me. I feel freed from the obligation of ever bringing her and her craziness around my children and family. I will no longer feed or entertain feelings of obligation for which I was just a child myself and had no control of . . . and I will not let my past be an excuse for not being here in the present and fulfilling my moral duty as a wife and mother."*

When callers ask me how to cope with the dying or death of a parent, I routinely ask them if they have loved that parent. Most of the time people say, "Yes." Then I tell them that this is exactly what the word "bittersweet" describes. The blessing of having a beloved parent is obvious; that's what the sweet is about. The sadness felt when that parent is gone is the necessary price you pay for that love; that is where the bitter comes in.

If you haven't loved that parent, there is no sweet and there is no sadness. There is only the reckoning with the truth that what you never had . . . is permanent. However, as I always remind people, the world is filled with wonderful people who can love you and fill you up . . . IF you let them.

## Nice People
## Don't Get Angry (?!)

Many of you are afraid to be, much less look, angry. Perhaps you were threatened or punished for angry outbursts when you were younger. Perhaps you don't want to further damage the disaster you're in. Perhaps you worry that your anger will eliminate better future possibilities. Whatever the reason, marinating in anger without resolve or appropriate expression is an unhealthy state of mind.

Diana called my program wanting to resolve the anger she has toward her mother, while at the same time having terrible guilt for being angry in the first place. I asked her first to look at the definition of guilt: a reaction from inside that lets you know that you're doing something wrong. People often misuse the word "guilt," when instead they are experiencing entirely different feelings.

If you are justifiably angry, it's not guilt you're feeling, it is more likely fear of punishment or further loss. You're not doing anything wrong by being justifiably angry. And the truth is, you probably aren't feeling guilt. It is more likely a pain of loss, a mourning of a hope never met; it is a potpourri of longing and of not wanting to do anything to eliminate the possibility of being lovingly mothered. But the reality is, and that is what you are angry about, that it'll never be. You haven't accepted it.

After I explained all of that to Diana, she was still felt emotionally stuck and wanted to know how to "deal with" her mother, whether or not she should talk to her.

I wondered aloud if there were something her mother could do right now to change history. Diana said, "No, she can't," but offered that something positive might happen if her mother apologized.

You'll remember that earlier I talked about the superiority of *acknowledgment* over *apologies*. Apologies can be exercises in lip service, but an acknowledgment of responsibility for the truth of your painful victimization or suffering goes a long way toward making you feel validated, your feelings justified, and your hard work in "getting yourself together" appreciated.

I suggested to Diana that she approach her mother and request *the truth* (starting with the impact of no bio-dad and four more stepdads and divorces) so that she might have an easier time letting go of her anger and so that they might start having a better quality of relationship, ". . . without," as Diana said, "me eating out my insides."

Of course, the challenge is accepting in advance that her mother might not be remorseful at all, or willing to demonstrate maternal compassion and basic humility. In that case, Diana will have to decide whether the walking-on-tulip-petal-approach, basically catering to her mother to have some semblance of a mother-daughter relationship, is really healthy and worth it.

DIANA: This is going to be difficult.
DR. LAURA: Oh, and the life you've been leading so far isn't?
DIANA: She's been the only parent I've had.
DR. LAURA: Yeah, well, you know what? You have a husband and kids, friends, and other relatives who love you and treat you well. That you've been hanging onto her with a synthetic relationship for emotional sustenance instead of reveling in these other alternatives is kind of sad.
DIANA: You're right, Dr. Laura. Okay. I'm going to have to get myself together here and see what I can do.
DR. LAURA: It's very easy. It's only twenty-two words:

"Mom, I need you to acknowledge to me the truth of what my life has been because of your decisions and actions."

DIANA: Okay, I'll give that a try.

As I always say on my radio program, "There is no trying; there is only doing."

### But What About When My Mom/Dad Is Mentally Ill?

In addition to tiptoeing around tulip petals to avoid losing what little you have with a difficult parent, there is the issue of how much compassion and slack you give a parent who is "mentally ill." Sheila called my show with just such a question. She wanted to know how to deal with the guilt that she felt about the last years with her mother, who had a lot of mental problems.

SHEILA: She ate me up and spit me out after my father died and basically brought out the worst in me. But still, I feel I should have been kinder, and more patient in a really impossible situation. I can't seem to put that away.

DR. LAURA: Once we look at the overall reality, we can ask, "How does a human being deal with this?" The answer probably is: the best they can, and at times, not that well. Were you brutal or cruel?

SHEILA: Oh, no.

DR. LAURA: You got impatient sometimes. I call that a human response. Now the only way we could have avoided a human response, Sheila, was to make you a robot.

SHEILA: I hear what you're saying and it sure makes sense ...

but then I go into the details. It's just that I feel sorry for her. She was a tortured soul.

DR. LAURA: I agree you should feel sorry for her. That doesn't mean her cruelty and torturing of you should go "not reacted to."

SHEILA: And you don't excuse somebody for being mentally ill?

DR. LAURA: If she was mentally ill to the degree of having no comprehension of right or wrong and no control over her behavior because she is not in our reality, what can I say? But the truth more likely is that she knew exactly what she was doing and she vented more with you because you were safer to vent with.

SHEILA: Yeah.

DR. LAURA: I bet if the postman walked in, she wouldn't have done "it" to him.

SHEILA: No, you're right.

DR. LAURA: I call that evil, and you probably don't want to believe that her behavior could have had intent—because it's too unbearable a thought. If she were not in charge of her faculties, then you'd feel better because "it wasn't personal," right? I think it's easier for you to accept that you're bad than the thought that she was intentionally cruel to you. You bought some of her crap, blaming you for her actions.

SHEILA: Yes, I did.

DR. LAURA: That's what I'm hearing now: "My mother was right! I'm bad." Well, Sheila, your mother was wrong— you're not bad, you're damaged.

SHEILA: How do you deal with when you know there were times when she was good and loving, but those times were less and less over the years?

DR. LAURA: You are a fifty-two-year-old child who wanted nothing more than to have a mother love her. Instead, you got this cruel, irrational, hurtful woman. And you are blaming yourself for not handling it like you were some kind of inanimate object. Sheila, THAT'S NUTS!

SHEILA: (laughing) Well, I thank you.

It is definitely not that I don't believe in compassion and understanding for parents who suffer from psychotic disorders and who therefore relate only to a made-up world filled with terrors and threats. I do. And I have helped many callers distinguish between parents being evil from those who are just plain annoying when they are attempting to categorize and cope with their parents' hurtful actions and words.

I have also instructed many an adult caller to discount the words and actions of a parent clearly incapacitated by serious organic brain diseases (as sometimes occur in old age), where sexual acting out, rage, and violence may often be the result of serious medical issues. However, these turn out to be the exceptions, not the rule.

I have often dealt with folks just not wanting to believe that evil behavior exists. It does. Evil is not a "condition" worthy of compassion. Of course, when you accept the reality of evil, it eliminates the possibility of you being responsible and having any potential control or influence over that parent. The mind-set of being responsible for your parent's bad treatment of you gives you hope that you can then make it be different. That hope is lost when you acknowledge evil; evil is an entity over which you have no control.

If you've watched a lot of teenage slasher or horror movies, you probably think of evil as supernatural-like, bloody, or extremely violent. Most evil, though, is mundane. It is not only the mother who says she is keeping the molester of her children in her home because the kids are lying or exaggerating, or it was a mistake and won't happen again, or she's just trying to keep a family together; it is the mother who makes a chubby daughter stay in a back room when company visits because she's embarrassed. It is not just the father who beats his children because he's frustrated with his life; it is the father who tells his son that he's a complete disappointment because he's artistic instead of macho, and wishes aloud that he were never born. It is not just the parents who abandon their children by the side of the road; it is also the parent who brainwashes the child to make false accusations of sexual or physical abuse against the other parent in a child custody case.

Are all bad parents evil? "Bad" implies that parents make conscious decisions to do things they know are not good for their kids out of basic self-centeredness, laziness, cowardice, and stubbornness. I believe those parents who, whether they admit to it or not, recognize that their actions are not in the best interests of their children, and who continue along with behaviors like:

- alcohol and drug abuse
- promiscuity (self-absorbed in their erratic love/sex life and exposing their children to risky and/or unstable situations)
- virtual abandonment (unnecessary nannies/day care/ babysitters/alone, frivolous divorces—minimal contact with their children while they remarry and have new children)
- insensitivity to the unique qualities, personality, and needs of their children (using their children for glory, financial gain, or ego gratification)

- negligence (ignore health issues of diet and exercise, resist appropriate medical treatment, lax supervision, nonparticipatory in educational process, virtual denial of child's problems, refusal of important extracurricular activities)
- lack of protection against abusive behaviors of lovers/spouses/relatives

are perpetrating evil acts on their children.

But the question still remains, are all *bad* parents *evil?* Frankly, that's a tough one to answer simply. I would have to put on a continuum the gradations from evil acts to a definitively evil person. A parent is evil if he or she derives benefit or pleasure from the suffering of their child, and has virtually no guilt, shame, or compassion for the suffering. That benefit or pleasure could be sexual arousal, feelings of superiority and power, vengeance against someone else (like the other parent), release from responsibilities (through abandonment, child selling or pimping, or murder), reduction of personal emotional distress (through violence or torture), and so forth.

Frankly, I think this distinction ultimately is not relevant. The evil acts speak for themselves; what you wish to call the perpetrator parent (unwitting, weak, cavalier, crazy, possessed, or evil) doesn't change the reality of the suffering children.

When the victims of some of these adult "evildoing" parents, their children, call my radio show feeling any sense of obligation to that parent, I routinely tell them that their mother or father has long since torn up their parent card. When a parent is dangerous or destructive, their presence should be minimized or eliminated altogether. People have a right to self-defense.

### Hey, I'm Not to Blame—I Did My Best!

Many a parent, confronted later in life, has come out with the excuse, "You just have to understand that I did my best at the time." For many parents, that's the truth. Christopher Reeve did the best he could to father his children from the confines of a paralyzed body. The wives of slain firemen, policemen, and military men generally do their very best to tend to the needs of their children as widowed parents. Parents with modest intellectual capabilities usually do their best to help their children with academics. What all these and other such parents have in common is that they indeed do their best, while circumstances—not their bad or irresponsible choices—limited them from being all they could have been without those externally imposed conditions.

Then there are those parents who try to justify some aspect of bad parenting by whitewashing history and excusing themselves from responsibility by proclaiming that their efforts were their best.

One listener, Russ, related to me his personal experiences with this situation. Russ is a thirty-eight-year-old happily married man with no children. His parents were divorced when he was around twelve, and he did not have much contact with his father after that. When he was twenty-four, he moved to the same town in which his dad was living and they started attending counseling together in an attempt to develop a closer relationship.

*"At our first meeting, I got very emotional from all the pain and hurt from the years of absence on his part, and he calmly replied, 'Son, you just have to understand that I did my best at the time.' Looking back, we had a bad counselor, and I left that session thinking that I must've done something wrong and that I was wrong for*

*feeling the pain and hurt that I was. I was also involved in quite a lot of self-destructive behavior prior to this first counseling session as well. Specifically, I was a heavy drug and alcohol user. I left that session feeling worse about myself than when I went in."*

*"To conclude, in the years following that, I have learned that his answer was really just an attempt to justify his actions, when in actuality, he had just done what he wanted to and what was easy for him with no regard for the family. Through your insights, Dr. Laura, as well as the love and support of my wife, I have come to realize that I didn't do anything to warrant his abandonment. My life is wonderful today. I gave up drugs and alcohol years ago and serve others any way I can."*

When parents call me on my radio program to "explain themselves" as part of their questions to me about their damaged relationships with their children, they often use that argument of the "best I could do." I ask them to explain to me what prevented them from, for example, seeing their child after a divorce. When I get back, "Well, my new spouse was from a different city," or "Well, my ex was difficult to deal with," or my personal favorite, "Well, it was so hard on me emotionally," I let 'em have it with both barrels: "Your child has a right to be angry. You did not concern yourself with his/her welfare, only your own impulses or desires. You made life easier for yourself and sacrificed your child."

"What do I do now?" they might ask.

"Admit to your wrongdoing, identify and acknowledge your weaknesses, admit to your self-centeredness. Tell them you were wrong and 'did them bad.' When you validate their reality and tell the truth, it opens up possibilities for a benevolent tomorrow between you. If you keep excusing yourself and making yourself the victim when in fact your behavior victimized your child, you keep the fight going. Until you are willing to go 'belly-up' you make your child have to fight you to corroborate the truth of their lives. Then there is no forward movement, no future, and no peace. Don't go there."

Of course, it's sometimes quite difficult to get people to own up to the truth of their own shortcomings. Nonetheless, it is the most benevolent gift a parent who has hurt their child can give.

## Why Am I Driving Myself Crazy?

I had a fascinating conversation with a caller, Jody, who told me straight up front that she has a tendency to try to be so perfect and to have everything a certain way. She was driven to call because of what I had said to a prior caller. I had told that other caller, semi-jokingly, "Perhaps all your physical health problems are nature's way of tapping you on the shoulder and telling you to slow down and treat yourself better. Since you're not listening, you keep getting tapped!"

Jody wanted my help. Evidently, she gets up at 4:30 in the morning to exercise, get herself ready and then get her kids ready for school. Since I get up at 5:30 A.M. to work out, take a three-mile walk to breakfast with my husband and puppy, and so forth, that just didn't seem too nutty to me!

DR. LAURA: So, what's wrong with that?
JODY: Nothing, but . . .
DR. LAURA: Then why do we have to change that?
JODY: I feel like my health has to be perfect; I have to look perfect before I walk out the door.

I asked her to take her cordless phone and walk me around her house. I asked her to start telling me the things that she notices that aren't perfect.

JODY: The bathroom. There's ... well, I'm injured now, so I haven't been able to do the things that I want to. I don't like to ask for help. So, it's not as clean as I want.

DR. LAURA: Describe the problem in your bathroom.

JODY: Okay, there is hair on the floor.

DR. LAURA: Whose hair?

JODY: Oh, mine, my kids ...

DR. LAURA: You mean you're losing your hair on top of everything else?

JODY: I know. Isn't that sad?

DR. LAURA: Stress will do that.

JODY: The tub needs to be scrubbed ... and I can't do it ... I'm injured!

DR. LAURA: So, you had to get injured in order to have a normal life?

JODY: Yes.

(both laughing)

I then asked her to take me back to who told her that she was lazy and stupid. Without much of a beat, she said, "My mother."

JODY: Well, I haven't spoken to her in eight years because of some things that she has done to me.

DR. LAURA: Okay, you are eight years old—tell me what it is like in your home.

JODY: Okay ... I would wet my bed and my face was rubbed in it. I was told I was dumb—constantly.

Dr. Laura: Yep, and it still hurts, doesn't it?

Jody: Yeah.

Dr. Laura: You're now forty-two. We have time to fix this. I just looked it up and you're going to live to be 97.5. This is going to seem a little strange, but try to stay with me on this. You're basic problem is that you are not angry.

Jody: Really?

Dr. Laura: Really. Let me explain something. When we're fearful and hurting because of a parent's abuse or rejection, there are a number of things that we can do, which you will recognize from your own life. We can cry and withdraw, or try to solicit Mom and Dad to like us. Differentiate that from being angry, saying, 'Screw you. You're a wacko and a bad mother.' Most children and young adults would have a lot of trouble saying that. And I don't necessarily mean that you have to say that to her. In fact, I don't think that is even necessary.

But here's Jody, spending most of her adult life trying to prove her mother wrong. But, alas, there are always hairs on the floor—there's always some proof that your mother was right. At least, that's how you interpret the hairs on the floor.

Jody: (whispering) . . . Oh my God!!!

Dr. Laura: So the transition you need to make, and I pray that you can do this because you will be most relieved, is to do things for the joy of doing them, instead of with the pain of trying to prove your mother wrong in your own mind. Your whole life is dedicated to that, which means you bought into her crap. And, my dear Jody, not talking to her didn't stop you from trying to prove her wrong, did it?

Jody: No—and I sure did buy it. Wow.

I went on to instruct her to shift from compulsive perfectionist to justifiably angry. As a joke, I did tell her that she'd have to do that . . . perfectly. Well, we had a good laugh.

What makes it so difficult for many damaged people to admit that they are angry with a parent or parents? Simple: anger is aggressive. Aggression scares most people, whether from others or from inside ourselves. It is really scary for most people to imagine taking on their parents in the privacy of their own heads, much less in person! You probably imagine even more punishment or rejection. And, sadly, you may have bought into their crap just enough to doubt yourself. It is that self-doubt, that possibility that you're not really lovable, that keeps you hanging onto the hope that you can someday, in some way, redeem yourself. It's my job to pull you out of that perpetual vortex.

In Jody's case, without her even being aware of it, she was pushing herself to perfection to prove that the abusive, mean, cruel, destructive things her mother did and said to her were not truly a reflection of her. She couldn't use her rational IQ to discern a mean mother from an inadequate child. That's how blinded you can be by your pain and fear.

Sometimes that concern about the judgment of a difficult parent gets turned into a compulsion to please everybody—whether they deserve it or not.

Samantha called my program with that issue. She constantly grapples with an intense feeling of concern for what other people are feeling. When she imagines that they're not happy, her assumption is that it has something to do with her. She criticizes herself for being self-centered, in that she is persistently worried about what others think about her.

Dr. Laura: I'm just wondering . . . it seems maybe too psychologically obvious, but . . . when you were little did you feel like you weren't certain about either your mom and/or your dad's love for you?

Samantha: Yes.

Dr. Laura: Tell me about that.

Samantha: They were divorced and my dad was not around and when he was he was really, really depressed and I was always sort of trying to make him happy and my mom is an addict.

Dr. Laura: Hmmm.

Samantha: I mean, I definitely sort of see the connection . . . but then I don't know how to stop it.

Dr. Laura: Yes, seeing it and feeling it are two different levels. You're hurting. Children grow up big and strong only when you give them the proper nutrients and they get exercise. It is the same with psyches and souls. You had two parents who were not parents. You never got what I tell people that their children need to get from them. You had two parents who did not behave like you meant something to them. You didn't learn to trust, you didn't learn your value, and you didn't learn to bond healthily. Your idea of bonding is to take care of them—them being anybody—hoping they'll want to stay.

Samantha: Yes! That is it, exactly! It is! Yeah, that's true.

I went on to describe herself to her, telling her that she's good at feeling everybody else's pain because it is easier than feeling her own. She wanted a quick fix, and I told her that I'd be glad to bop her over the head with my magic wand, but that I'd left it at home that day.

A typical response, one given by Samantha, to the understanding that you have a habit pattern of treating all new situations as though they were a reincarnation of you and your parent(s) is "I feel this is a childish thing, ridiculous, and I ought to be able to just stop it."

DR. LAURA: Well, you know, the more you keep being snotty about yourself, the less you're going to allow yourself to feel your own pain. I mean, every time you describe this situation, you are mean to yourself! You're the injured party. It's a real injury, not a bratty thing. You were starved and you're undernourished in an area that never developed properly: the area which allows you to see others as other than entities to let you know you're okay.

It is important to recognize that when you are continually taking everyone's emotional temperature to make sure you are still okay with respect to them, you are in fact being very self-centered. It looks as though you are concerned about their feelings, but in reality, your concern is ultimately only for your own safety in the relationship.

The magic fix, if there were one, would have the following elements:

- a recognition and acceptance that your pattern of feeling, thinking, and behaving is stuck in the broken-record reality of your childhood painful circumstances
- a mourning for the healthy, loving family situation you never had (truth and tears)
- a commitment to change, no matter how scary
- a greater focus on your loving, caring behaviors toward others—without the obligatory "Am I okay?"

It is the final step that makes the big difference in your life. It is a requirement to behave *as if* you had received all the love, affection, support, nurturance, peace, and sanity that every childhood ought to provide. It is in the effort to come away from yourself that you "grow up" into an adult. You see, while you're stuck in the past, you are largely childlike in your perceptions, reactions, and behaviors. As I tell my listeners, behaviors drag feelings forward. If you wait for the miracle of all your feelings to become mature, get yourself a rocking chair so that you can be comfortable in your old age as you wait for that miracle.

### Don't Touch Me!

Of course, the flip side to being a people pleaser is being a speck in the distance, making sure you're not close enough to get hurt . . . or at least that's the logic you believe explains your pattern of behavior.

Krista called me about wanting to change that kind of pattern in her life, staying just enough distance away from people to protect herself. The part that bothers her the most is that she's been married for almost four years, and it keeps her from being really close to her husband.

I asked her, "What was the worst thing that could come from getting close to someone?" Her answer was that her deepest fear is that they would take a chunk out of her and she'd never get it back, and she'd lose who she was or was trying to be. I remarked that in reality, "No one has that power; they can humiliate, hurt, or betray you, but they can never take away from you who you are."

KRISTA: Well, if it was a person you cared about and respected . . .

DR. LAURA: Ahh. You mean to say that if someone you depended upon emotionally was critical of you for something, you'd have to change that—thereby losing yourself?

Her answers seemed bizarre and unrelated to my questions, like she was taking me on some merry race. Perhaps I had gotten too "heady," because at this point in the conversation I felt I had lost the connection with her. It's ironic that she came on telling me she had a hard time getting or staying close to others and being vulnerable—and in just a few minutes together, I felt disconnected. Fortunately, we had a commercial break at that moment! Saved by the commercial!

During the break I tried to just clear my mind of my theories and potential comebacks to what she'd already said. I just let my consciousness flow, hoping in a strange way to have it merge with hers. In the span of thirty years of doing this radio program, I have come to trust that instinct.

Nonetheless, I surprised myself with what I said to Krista immediately upon coming back. I just had this odd sense that she wasn't really protecting *herself* at all.

DR. LAURA: Krista, who is it you'd really like to hurt? Who is it you've always wanted to really hurt? Who is that person?

KRISTA: (long silence) My mother.

[I hope you readers are impressed. Frankly, my mind was blown!]

DR. LAURA: You want to flesh that out a bit?

KRISTA: Sure. I used to have dreams where I was actually

physically hitting her and nothing impacted her at all. And that's kind of the way our relationship used to be. I can't say it's that way now, because I've chosen to accept the reality of that relationship.

DR. LAURA: Not *exactly*. What you have done is controlled yourself from killing her—literally and figuratively. And the way you've done that is to shut yourself off—period.

KRISTA: What do you mean, "from killing her"?

DR. LAURA: I don't think I have to clear that one up. You are so afraid of that piece of you that is full of rage and could "kill her," or somebody else who hurts you, you just shut it all off because you don't trust you. You are scared of what you are capable of.

KRISTA: I'm scared that I'll hurt someone who gets close of me because of all that rage? Well, my husband can probably attest to that. I think I already do that. When I do my best at not hurting him, we're not that close. Trying to protect everyone is still hurting them because I'm not close.

I went on to tell her that I didn't imagine she was really capable of what she most worried she'd do, that she is too decent, kind, and loving a person. I told her that it was okay for her to get angry with important people in her life, without worrying that the rage she has for her mother would spill over into hurting them.

I sent her off to think about all of this and to call me back. She called me about ten days after this conversation.

KRISTA: You told me that I needed to mull over that idea of the fact that I was not really capable of doing that; that the person I am is not capable of doing that. And I did mull. And I had a good cry. But after that, I felt a little bit of weight lifting. And I truly do believe that I was not trusting myself.

[Blessed BINGO!]

KRISTA (continued): I found that I've been able to handle some pretty tough things with my husband and not be terrified. I'm responding differently to him but he still thinks that I'm, you know, manipulating when I am angry or annoyed. I'm telling him more of what the true reasons are as to why I'm upset. I'm communicating, not manipulating.

I told her that it would take time for them both to adjust to more openness and intimacy with clearer, more honest communication. Patience is always required when changes are being made. After that phone call, I said to the listening audience, "There's somebody moving forward and feeling more peace."

### Who Am I?

Krista's problem was not really knowing and trusting herself. That is not an unusual problem for people who have had Bad Childhoods. Bad Childhoods get in the way of you developing a clear picture of yourself and an understanding of your impulses, needs, and fears, with a healthy set of controls.

Amber called my program because she has an ". . . enormous amount of resentment and anger toward my mother."

She wanted to know how she could get rid of that because it is ". . . consuming my life."

The first thing I did was to make her prove to me that this was, indeed, consuming her life. I asked if she weren't sleeping or eating properly, not working, unable to have any fun, and so forth. After that challenge she pulled back from her position. This is important, because exaggeration convinces even ourselves that we're worse off than we are, in addition to providing drama for attention. Once you tone down your own rhetoric in describing yourself or your life, you will already demonstrate to yourself that you're coping better than you know.

Of course, for those who fear life more than they fear the pain they're so familiar with, that's a negative outcome.

Getting into Amber's story revealed that she once had a good relationship with her mom. When Mom divorced Dad seven years ago because he was an alcoholic, things changed.

DR. LAURA: What did she do that was so bad? Your father was a drunk and you're not telling me you're mad at him.

AMBER: Well, I'm dealing with that, too. But my mother moved us three times and married someone that we hated. She puts him and his children in front of us.

DR. LAURA: Well, that's a worthy thing to be angry over.

AMBER: I don't want to be angry anymore.

DR. LAURA: First, it's reasonable to be angry. Your father was a drunk. And your mother is a very weak, dependent, not too thoughtful or circumspect kind of woman. You are a unique human being. And as such, you have possibilities, potential, and the opportunities to express them—to do wonderful things with your life.

So, on the one hand, it's perfectly reasonable to be angry and disappointed at two parents who didn't do their jobs well. On the other hand, you still have this unique life with which to do something positive and rewarding. If you're going to put that aside to marinate in your justifiable anger, then you're not doing what you're supposed to be doing with your life—which makes you very much like your mother and father!

It doesn't matter what reason we have for wasting your lives—the point is that we're wasting it. So your challenge is to use your unique qualities to the best advantage for the world and you. There is something special you have to offer, in spite of the fact that your launchpad was cracked.

AMBER: (laughing)

DR. LAURA: But you can still go out into the universe, even from a cracked launchpad. I can't take away your pain, you'll have that for the rest of your life. Your disappointments over being virtually an orphan . . . you can't do anything about those facts. Ugly, yucky facts. Now, you're not going to be able to do wonderful things with your life if you constantly think about yourself and present yourself as "a life being consumed by this enormous hate!"

That cracked launchpad is a part of you—not all of you. Let's see what Amber can do with a life in spite of two flaky parents.

AMBER: Okay.

Here is the universal message I hope was well expressed through Amber's call:

1. Yeah, you're upset—and to some extent you always will be.
2. Don't waste your life on it, though—fight it. Don't grab your own ankles while you're running up the stairs.

## Who Can Contain My Pain?

So many of you who have had Bad Childhoods have a lot of anger. My advice is to do healthy things with your life in spite of that pain. The question does remain, "How do I cope with the pain/anger?" The healthy ways include quality therapy, sports, hobbies, yoga, work, charity work, and so forth. In this way you distract yourself and sublimate those powerful emotions into positive outlets.

Carol wrote to me about one more outlet.

*"I heard you tell a caller she had a lot of rage she needed to deal with. That certainly struck a chord!*

*"Over twenty years ago, I was diagnosed with depression. When my therapy sessions first started, I 'accepted' what had happened in my childhood. The doctor seemed to be trying to make me mad, and I couldn't figure out why and resisted. He asked me why I didn't seem upset about what had happened to me. I told him I know people who had suffered worst and I certainly didn't want to wallow in self-pity. He kept pushing, asking me again why I didn't get mad about all I had gone through. Did I think I deserved it? No, but why get angry, it wouldn't change anything.*

*"He asked if I was mad at God about what I had gone through. Oh no, I couldn't be angry at God. He wanted to know why not? Because I was Catholic and it is wrong to get mad at God.*

*"Then he asked me the question that finally broke through and allowed me to start the grieving process and move forward: 'WHO BETTER TO HANDLE YOUR ANGER THAN GOD?' God could handle it. God could deal with all my rage when people around me might not be able to.*

*"So, I yelled at God (forgetting about the doctor and talking just to God) and asked 'Why me? It isn't fair!' And I told Him everything that I was afraid to show anyone else about how MAD I truly*

*was. I literally screamed and cried until I was exhausted and done telling Him how I felt.*

*"When I was done, the doctor looked at me and said, 'OK, now you can start putting it behind you.'*

*"I later thanked God for letting me take it out on Him. I didn't even want to admit to myself how mad I was (a feeling that once I starting ranting and raving, I wouldn't be able to stop) but was safe in giving the hurt and anger to Him.*

*"I put the hurt away in the very back of my heart and mind . . . and moved on."*

And you can, too.

# SIX

# Never Seek Love from the Devil

*My advice is to never give in to evil. Never let yourself become the bad experiences inflicted upon you in your childhood. Try to transcend and learn from the negative, turning those experiences into something good, true and right. Most importantly, trust in God. I am living proof that right can overwhelm wrong.*

**—Robert, a listener**

When Robert was eleven, his father's birthday present for him was a big bundle of about thirty switches, three- to four-feet-long elm tree cuttings from his yard, tied up with a red ribbon. His father, an elementary school teacher, beat Robert, as he had done daily, with each and every switch, only shifting to a new one when one broke. Robert's mother never interceded, never called police or child protective services, and never left.

The beatings stopped when Robert was fifteen and big enough to defend himself. He fought off a beating one day by pinning his father in a wrestling move he'd learned in eighth-grade gym class the year before. His father was hu-

159

miliated, and just a few days later filed for divorce and left. The family was free of the devil.

Robert was determined to make a success of his life, in spite of his traumatic childhood. He wanted to become the kind of a father he never had growing up: good, kind, and loving. To succeed as a father, he used his own father as the contrast. *"When in doubt, I did everything the exact opposite of my own father. I was successful as evidenced by the positive proof of my beautiful boys telling their friends that I was an excellent father to them."*

This is a great outcome for a horrendous situation. While it is obvious that his father was evil, it may not be obvious that his mother was even more so. For any parent, any adult for that matter, to stand by and watch the virtual torture of children and not act on their behalf is unconscionable—and evil.

I hear from adults all the time on my radio program who share horror stories of one parent sexually molesting them or a sibling, brutal beatings, outrageously vicious harangues, negligence, or exhibiting dangerous behaviors like driving drunk with kids in the car or leaving children alone, and on and on, while the other parent does nothing to protect them. Often they have formed some sort of relationship with the "stander-by," mostly for the sake of not being a complete orphan. Nonetheless, I tell them that this allegiance and alliance is sick and self-destructive. And the ugly consequences are far-reaching.

After hearing a call I took on my radio program with a woman who said she could not love herself, her son, or her husband due to the abuse she suffered as a child by her father—which, by the way, both her parents refused to admit to—Patty, a listener wrote: *"You told her to tell them to drop dead and then never see them again. This was a very hard call, but with your loving* guidance, and a courageous caller, you guided her to a potentially life-changing decision.

"I related to almost everything in the call, but what really grabbed my attention and made the most impact was when you said to her, 'Never, ever seek love from the Devil.' Wow!! That is what I have struggled with for fifty-one years, but never before was it put in such plain words. As a spiritual woman, that is something I can really recognize and begin to deal with.

"I grew up in a very abusive childhood. I never thought of myself as beaten until I was well into my forties. The physical abuse was called spankings, and all my friends were spanked, so I thought it was normal. Only later did I learn that spanking a five to ten-year-old child to the point of causing the child to pass out were beatings. And I also learned that spanking a teenager with belts, sticks, hangers, and ropes after stripping the child nude, was not only a beating, but sexual abuse.

"But instead of confronting my parents as an adult, I remained the scared child trying to win their approval until both of them passed away. And what did that cost me? It cost me thirty years of my adult life, living as a scared child, choosing two abusive husbands, and letting my daughter grow up thinking it was OK to abuse me."

Here is where the story gets even more intense. Patty's nineteen-year-old son is loving, respectful, an A student, pre-med, lettered in various sports, and a self-taught violinist. Patty's thirty-year-old daughter has fabricated lies about beatings, sexual harassment, and rapes (she's been arrested for false rape charges) by everybody else in her path, including her mother, for almost two decades. She even accused Patty of abusing her child during the time Patty and her new husband brought them into the home because, after accusing her employer of one week of harassment, she had no place to go. Patty, trying to be a good mother, has continued to jump through hoops trying to help and stay connected.

Finally, her new husband (the one good guy in the picture so far) warned her to be careful what she wished for. He reminds her that her daughter is a liar, narcissistic, domineering, moody, rude, sadistic, and dangerous considering her lies about Patty's "criminal acts" of abuse toward her and the grandson. This was, of course, nothing Patty wanted to hear. Of course Patty has guilt about her daughter's childhood. Of course Patty has guilt about her own weaknesses. Of course Patty has guilt about not having the magic to make her daughter more positively functional. Of course, therefore, Patty didn't want to give up. She's a mother.

*"But, you know what?—After today and your show, maybe my eyes are open. Finally! I have spent all my life seeking love from the Devil. And maybe this time, I can do what is right for me and the rest of my family. My son even tells me that I take too much away from the family being sad and obsessed with my daughter. And now I understand. I couldn't really hear him until your show today. I GET IT!*

*"I have a wonderful marriage with a loving, supportive husband now, so I have stopped seeking romantic love from a Devil. But it is time that I stop hurting and living as a scared child from the pain my parents caused and it is time I stopped trying to get love from my abusive daughter. It is time to give the real adult to my family and even to myself.*

*"THANK YOU, THANK YOU, THANK YOU!!!"*

"Never, ever seek love from the devil." I have had to say that phrase innumerable times on my radio program to people who:

- seem mesmerized by their fantasies of a lovely relationship with somebody who is, frankly, horrible

- imagine a magical purging of the pain from their sad history
- are in incredible denial
- don't have the courage to face the unpredictability of their lives moving forward
- have so much fear of confronting the "devil" that they are emotionally immobilized

It is understandable that you would want to hold on as long as possible and do whatever it takes to have a warm, loving relationship with a parent because you imagine that then you would be at peace. But acceptance of reality is the only true pathway to peace.

Emily wrote to me about her father. He had cheated on and abused her mother for years. When her parents finally separated, her sisters refused to live with Mom because they were mad at her for leaving Dad. Emily is the only one who stayed with Mom. Sadly, all the sisters were beaten and sexually molested and came back to live with Emily and her mother after one year.

Court cases ensued because Dad was suing them for "everything." She felt very cheated by an evil, dangerous father—instead of having a loving, protective daddy—and by a court system that didn't ultimately protect them. When in high school, she met and dated a boy wiser than his years. He helped her get through her problems and seemed to have a clear mind on what was right and wrong. When she would waver with need and longing for "a father," her boyfriend would say, *"Why would you want to be around a man like that?"*

She ended up marrying him, but the weight and shadow of her need for her father to love her, to be involved in her life, kept her focused on her sick yesterday, rather than her potential tomorrow; consequently, she ignored her husband and marriage and stayed focused on her dad.

*"I had to learn the hard way that my father had not changed. I started listening to Dr. Laura on the radio. One day a guy called in with a situation like mine. He was asking if he should contact his father. After listening to his description of his father's vicious behaviors, Dr. Laura said, 'Why would you want to have a relationship with the devil?' He said, 'He is my father.' Dr. Laura said, 'OK, why would you want a relationship with your father-devil?' Right then it hit me. When I was 14 years old, and ended the relationship the first time, I said to my dad, 'When I am around you I feel confusion, and that is from the devil. When I am with my mom I feel peace, and that is from God.'*

*"Right then, I asked myself, why do I want a relationship with the devil? I don't! Ever since I confronted myself with that question, I have felt better."*

*"So, go on with your life, and try to stay happy. You will have a better relationship with your spouse, and the people who love and care about you."*

And now I come back to the issue of "victims" becoming myopic if not entirely self-absorbed. I know, I know—you feel like I'm kicking the horse after it's down. No, actually, I'm encouraging it to stand up and take care of the colts!

One listener wrote to me about feeling like she was in a time tunnel, hearing a call on my program that sounded like something out of her own life. The call she heard was from a nineteen-year-old daughter of divorced parents whose mother was incapable of loving despite a long-term marriage and five children. This listener's mother, now seventy-seven and in poor health, just like that teenage caller, only the year was 1943. Her mother's mom was a cold and calculating, eventually divorced mother of five children, her own mother being the second youngest and the apple of Daddy's eye—which made her the scapegoat of her mother's wrath, resulting in her being thrown out of the home as a minor!

*"My tender-hearted Mom spun a hopeless dream of finding her own mother's love and respect; a wasted effort that both blinded and drove her for decades. Having been warned by the father who she adored to avoid this entanglement, she jettisoned wisdom to try to net the impossible. My mom's marriage to my dad was strained and the fall-out also hit my sibling and me. Our little family lived in hardship to finance this basically self-serving and manipulative old woman who had long before driven sensible people away from her. My grandmother's ruthlessness battered the upcoming generation because my Mom opened the door to it.*

*"The clean break you wisely urged, Dr. Laura, upon your caller will be the toughest thing she's had to face because it requires maturity. In the process she'll realize that (1) she'll never be good enough, (2) that her mother won't change, and (3) that she risks her own future and those around her.*

*"Cutting away the evil before the tumor metastasizes into her home will save a family. Yesterday's pains dim in comparison. Having partly lived the effects of my mom not doing so, I know the pain and loss."*

This self-centeredness results in:

- allowing sexually or violently abusing relatives access to your children to maintain a sense of hope about having a relationship with them
- not standing by a person who was abused because you wish to benefit from a relationship with the abuser—after all, "you weren't abused"
- constantly marinating in past pain and staying involved in current turmoil with the abusive parent to the extent

166 Dr. Laura Schlessinger

that your mental and physical health are compromised and you end up neglecting or abusing your own family

This last behavior is a frequent one. Tom and Jayne called my program to discuss problems Tom perceives with Jayne's mother.

TOM: We're having problems with her mother. She has been interfering a lot. Her mom has done it to basically every one of her children.

JAYNE: She has tried to get us to divorce.

I asked Jayne why she chose to have contact with such a dangerous and destructive mother. The pattern was clear and not a function of Jayne's choice of a husband. At first Jayne just sighed. Then came all the smokescreen and denial.

JAYNE: I guess I didn't really realize what she was doing and the extent of it, and, ah, I don't want her to be the way she is. Because I love her, and I have kids that I want to have know her.

DR. LAURA: Jayne, that can't be a true statement.

JAYNE: I mean, she's not always a terrible person. She's helped us a lot, too. My mother was a really good mom. She's very controlling. She's loving.

DR. LAURA [here it comes!]: She's not a good, loving mom. You are lying.

JAYNE: 'Cause she's always been there for me all of my life.

DR. LAURA: She's not been there *for* you, she's *owned* you.

JAYNE: Well . . . yeah, you're probably right.

Jayne then went into lie number 2: "I just don't know what to do. I just don't know how to handle it."

DR. LAURA: That's a lie. You lie a lot. Jayne, is that how you handle your weakness? [Both Tom and Jayne laughed] She's a loving mother and you want your children to benefit from her warmth . . . and have their marriages destroyed by her? Really?

TOM: That's so true.

JAYNE: I think a lot of it has to do with probably when I was younger, because the fact that I didn't know any other families that had two parents other than mine. I always kind of had this perfection vision of my family, I guess, where everybody loved each other. We didn't have any drug addicts or alcoholics and nobody was beating anybody. You know, I just thought everything was fine.

DR. LAURA: Well, that's not exactly true either; now you're up to lie number 3. You've seen how destructive she was.

JAYNE: I know. And I see it a lot more now that I'm an adult. I see what she does to my father and my siblings and how she has controlled me. I understand she's doing that. But she's also my mother and has done things for me.

DR. LAURA: Actually, that doesn't really matter now, because the primary responsibility you have is to protect your husband and children.

TOM: Thank you!

JAYNE: Yeah, really. Do you think I should just stay away from her? Not talk to her?

DR. LAURA: If that's what it takes to protect your family, then that's what it takes.

JAYNE: Should I confront her?

DR. LAURA: I'm not sure that would change anything.

JAYNE: She won't change. I understand. It makes me sad. It makes me really sad.

DR. LAURA: Well, that's why you lie to yourself a lot—you don't want to feel the pain. You have been protecting yourself so long from pain that you make up stories about how deliriously perfect and happy everything is. You knew every moment that it was miserable—but you didn't want to know it, or feel the pain.

JAYNE: I understand, and I have to figure out how to come to terms with this. I just wanted to be part of a family.

DR. LAURA: You are; you created one. Tom's right there for you.

JAYNE: How do you know the line of what you accept and what isn't acceptable—people are imperfect.

DR. LAURA: This has nothing to do with imperfection. This has only to do with evil, and evil can be quite perfect, my dear. And when you want to know the line . . . look to Tom; watch the expression on his face.

JAYNE: Thank you very much. It's so true. It's so true. I wouldn't have put up with what he's put up with. And I've had to mature a lot and I feel really bad for the things that I have allowed my mother to do to us.

DR. LAURA: Now, go enjoy your husband and your children—and get rid of the demons.

There are times when a complete cutoff is the healthiest decision you could make. That cutoff may be temporary or permanent. You may choose to "check them out" at some point to discern whether or not they've learned and grown sufficiently to relate to you and your family in a healthy, nondestructive way. You may choose to "check yourself out"

at some point to discern whether or not you've grown sufficiently to be able to handle their liabilities without suffering.

Deborah, a listener, evolved to a point where she could
choose the latter option. Upon hearing my call with a young
woman whose destructive and manipulative mother just
played "suicide attempt," she wrote about her problematic relationships with both of her parents, but primarily with her
father. After bouts of severe depression when in her twenties,
she found a wonderful therapist who told her the following
story—which has stuck with her ever since:

"He said, 'If you put a mouse in a maze with cheese at the
end, they'll make it through the maze and eat the cheese. Then, if
you take the cheese away, or only put it in sometimes, the mouse
will go through the maze a couple more times, and then give up.
Humans, however, never give up looking for the cheese. We'll go
through that maze over and over and over, hoping for the cheese
and we won't give up no matter how many times we are hurt.'
Then he said to me, 'Stop looking for the cheese from your dad. It's
not there.'"

Deborah went on to describe how those words liberated
her. She didn't get hurt anymore by her dad's callous indifference. She stopped expecting and hoping for those shining
moments when he'd love her and everything would be right
with the world. In short, she got on with her life.

When she was thirty-five, she married. During the planning of her wedding, her father was amazingly helpful, both
emotionally and financially. She didn't trust it at first, and she
still doesn't expect it to continue for the rest of her life. She
realizes he still has issues, but "I am grateful for each small piece
of cheese I get from my dad. And all because I did exactly what you
suggested to a caller . . . I let him go. I did the same with my mom,
and while she is still as self-centered as ever, she does at least make

*the effort to maintain some semblance of a relationship with me—
which believe me, is a huge thing!"*

Some of you will be able to handle the limitations; others
of you would be better off with no contact. Don't jump into
the deep end of the pool when you can't even tread water. If
you can never get yourself to tread water, keep away from the
pool or you'll just keep filling your lungs with water and your
life will be a continuous experience of small emotional and
psychological drownings. Unfortunately, you'll drag too many
people down with you: your spouse, children, and friends as
they try to find a place in your heart for them when your heart
is all involved with your destructive parents. It's as though your
heart has a LOT FULL sign hanging over it.

So be honest about who you are and what you can do,
and be honest about what you're up against.

Linda wrote me an incredible letter relating a forty-one-
year journey in coming to peace with an alcoholic, drug-
abusing, violent mother and an absent, workaholic father
who just looked the other way. Linda tried to fix her mother
and salvage any relationship with her parents at all costs to
her and her family. She felt that because they were her parents they deserved her unconditional love. The only thing
that terminated her "trying" was her mother's death.

It took all this time, four decades of misery and hopeless
effort, and hearing a caller to my show regarding her difficulty in relating to the men in her life for her to let it go.

In that call, the woman acknowledged the core of her
problem: two evil parents. Linda wrote, *"My wish is anyone
who finds themselves in a similar situation, please listen and get as
far away from the evil as you can so you can diminish inevitable
heartbreak. As children, we all deserve to be happy and loved. Unfortunately, some of us need to learn quicker when love and/or ac-*

*ceptance by our parents is not possible. We must accept that we can achieve love through others."*

A listener sent me a quote he took from *Psychology Today* (Jeanne Safer, 2/05) that I thought was extremely brave because the typical psychotherapeutic mantra is that without forgiveness you cannot be healthy. "Contrary to the conventional wisdom," the quote begins, "refusing to forgive or have further contact with an unrepentant, abusive relative [or any individual, for that matter] is therapeutic." By now you know that I agree wholeheartedly with this. I can attest to the insight and relief so many people have expressed when they saw, from kind of a third-person position, the abuser for what he/she was. What sets in is a sense of indifference that can free you up.

I believe you can give up being angry without forgiving. I believe that being coerced to forgive is yet another abuse. I've seen families try to extort one sibling to "forgive" the abuse from another, all for the sake of so-called family harmony. I've seen people pushing themselves to forgive unrepentant abusers, in total denial of their just feelings and experiences, just so that they won't be labeled as, or feel like, the "bad one."

I believe that some acts are wholly unforgivable. Without having limits on the idea of forgiveness, victimized people are often depressed, easily manipulated, confused about what is right or wrong, and unclear as to which of their perceptions and opinions are real. There are simply acts that are worthy of tolerance, and others that aren't. Unfortunately, in dysfunctional homes those lines are blurred by the perpetrators—all must be accepted or else.

## When, Where, How, and What
## Is a "Healthy Kiss-Off"?

*"My name is Bella, and I am twenty-four years old,"* wrote Bella, a listener. Her father is, and always has been, struggling with being an alcoholic his whole life. *"Actually, I shouldn't say he has struggled—because he doesn't think it's a problem. I struggle with the pain it causes—not physical, but emotional pain—the disappointment of every broken promise, usually a promise to stop drinking. I even struggle with my own emotions, which range from loving him to death to hating him with a passion."*

Her father's drinking habits have resulted in three failed marriages and a broken relationship with Bella. She's always tried to keep things in perspective with respect to her dad, constantly trying to focus on the fact that he has a "problem" and "needs help." She's persistently put aside her own feelings of anger and frustration at the fact that *"I have to parent him, emotionally and financially."*

Evidently his twin brother committed suicide and his father died, both in the same year. His mother passed away also and he is always in a financial bind, not being able to pay his rent or make his monthly car payment. However, his drinking "problem" predated all of these events. Nonetheless, adult children like Bella, who are basically kind, compassionate and desperate to "fix the parent" so that they can have some semblance of a normal parent-child relationship, get caught up in the sympathetic moment and experience guilt for having negative feelings of holding that parent accountable for their own actions and reactions.

You probably also try to be understanding by excusing and rationalizing, protecting and rescuing a parent who is sucking out your soul. Perhaps you pay the bills to help them get "caught up," only to find that they negligently and cavalierly, definitely intentionally, screw up yet again—assuming you'll be there to bail them out again.

Bella did that; she'd give her father money, and, *"He ends up skipping work and getting drunk again, which outrages me because I know I'm being taken advantage of. I am sick and tired of worrying about him. I avoid calling or visiting him because I think he might be drunk, but he interprets my behavior as not caring enough. I know alcoholism is a disease and that it is very hard to quit without help, but he refuses to acknowledge that he has a problem and will not get help."*

There are a number of important issues here that I believe will help you emotionally and psychologically disengage from this type of destructive parent. First comes the question as to whether alcoholism/drug abuse, philandering, overeating, and lack of self-discipline are "diseases."

With third-party payment, for example, insurance company reimbursement, treatments have been devised and designed around calling numerous types of self-indulgent, bad behaviors and habits "diseases." Now, for example, a spouse who breaks his/her vows and fools around with other partners is a "sex addict" instead of a creep. I cannot tell you how many husbands and wives call me feeling guilty for wanting to get out of a marriage with a philanderer because some therapist has convinced them that their spouse is not morally corrupt and self-indulgent, but the victim of a disease! "They just can't help themselves." Outrageous! The only irresistible impulse is one that hasn't been resisted.

That people do "bad" things because they get "good vibes" from doing them is not a disease—it is a moral failing. There is no surgery, medication, or physical therapy that "cures" these ailments; they are "cured" by a commitment to

doing the right thing, and putting aside immediate gratification for the sake of principles, love, honor, and character. It
is difficult to give up self-focused, immediate gratification.
But that difficulty is inevitably outweighed by a longer-
term sense of peace. Basically, these are people who don't
care who they're hurting as long as they don't have to face
themselves.

When people, even someone you call Mommy or Daddy,
will not take responsibility for their dangerous and destructive behaviors, don't seem to have sensitivity to or guilt for
the havoc they wreak, and therefore refuse to take steps to
improve the situation, you need to start thinking seriously
about some degree of disconnect. If you don't, because of
guilt or because you just can't bring yourself to "give up,"
you'll probably find that your life is circumscribed around
their antics and not your own family or personal growth. You
are then virtually giving your life over to them, instead of
having one of your own.

Bella's letter continued with, *"I called him early this morning
to see how he was doing and he was drunk again—and so in that
moment of intense anger, I told him that I don't ever want to see or
hear from him again until he proves to me that he has stopped
drinking. Is it very selfish of me to expect him to quit for me if he
won't even do it for himself? Is it even realistic? I am in a predicament because I am really the only family he has and I don't want to
turn my back on him, but he turns his back on me every time he
drinks and I am truly tired of hurting. Please help me."*

My guess is that many of you identify will Bella's
"predicament," which is a sense of responsibility fighting dis-
gust, a sense of longing fighting rage. Your feelings are one
hundred percent justified. You've also tried to help—in fact,
you've probably also gone too far in your rescue attempts

and have probably given your parent or sibling more money, time, and effort than you can afford. You've put part of your life aside to dedicate time, effort, heart, and soul to a person who is completely unwilling to do anything for himself, much less for you.

So the question remains, "When do you give up?" I believe the answer is, "When it is clear that you are the cart trying to push the totally resistant horse forward," or, "When the horse's hooves are clearly destroying the cart behind it." It is sad and regrettable, but you've got to get out of the way—it's called self-defense. I have always believed that people have the responsibility to make sure they don't let someone else destroy them.

## Unresolved Rage Splashes Everywhere

It is the ability to control the level of actual involvement within the limits of your emotional and psychological limitations and strengths that will decide whether or not, or how much, you are able to handle with an awful parent. I therefore do not have a one-size-fits-all answer to the question of whether or not you should disconnect. It depends very much on where a parent's behavior falls on the continuum between evil to awful to annoying, and on your strength and ability to disengage emotionally when you have to accept the limitations of the situation. When you don't come to a place of equanimity in your heart and soul about the truth and limitations of what is possible to have with a difficult or awful parent, you are in constant internal turmoil and usually take it out on others, in addition to how much you allow yourself to continue to suffer. And as I will talk about in chapter seven, you do and can make decisions that ultimately change behaviors and then feelings.

Megan, a listener wrote: *"I just got done listening to the caller you had talking about how she has mistreated her husband and son because of her hatred of her parents and their awful behavior. Three years ago I was in her same shoes. I was nothing but hateful toward my children and husband and actually physically abusive toward my husband—how he has stood by me I'll never know.*

*"Most of this was due to my own self-hatred for 'putting up' with my mother and her abusive ways toward me. I too had been 'bought off' with her monetary help, but it always came with a price—a price I finally realized was too high.*

*"I finally told her off and told her she was no longer going to hurt me or my family, and that she was no longer welcome in my life. I told her that she had hurt me for thirty-two years and I was no longer going to put up with that and that I most certainly was not going to put up with her abuse toward my children and husband.*

*"I just hope that the woman who called you is listening to you, because it is so personally fulfilling to know that I stood up to my bully of a mother and that I am now a stronger, happier woman for taking control of my life. I was so out of control for SO long. I work with at-risk children, and I tell them often that unfortunately you can only be the best person YOU can, you can't help having crummy parents, and you can't help it sometimes that the world is not fair to you. YOU make your life happy, not someone else."*

What is it they say, "Poop rolls downhill"? Yes, indeed it does. So if you stay engaged in a bitter, fruitless struggle, accommodating an awful parent or sibling, trying to "make it work," your stress, rage, and need to finally feel in control WILL probably end up with you becoming awful to those who love you (spouses) and depend upon you (your children).

KG, a listener, wrote to me thanking me. She wanted to let me know that by listening to my radio program, she was guided down a long path toward positive change. With strength and conviction, she disengaged from her destructive mother. Since then, the frequent migraines (one to three per month) she's had since the age of four have completely stopped. *"I haven't had even a hint of one since."*

KG realized that trust is learned in childhood within the context of the mother-child relationship. While she did not learn trust then, she's caught up now, and is taking pleasure in caring for her family and striving to be the kindest, most loving, compassionate, strong, moral, trustworthy person in their lives.

I am always thrilled when people from Bad Childhoods are committed so intensely to breaking the cycle. It is of course great for their children, and it is a beautiful gift to give themselves: peace and the joy of a wonderful parent–child relationship.

When someone writes to me after we've spoken on my radio program, I am always anxious to know what they did with the experiences. Wendy, who signed herself "a listener for life," wrote to me after our call in which she asked if she should cut her mother out of her life now that she and her husband are expecting their first child. Wendy's mother was physically and mentally abusive and is still married to her stepfather, who sexually abused her. Wendy had never disconnected from her mother on any level.

When she called, as with so many other callers, she had the sense to know the answer. Nonetheless, and I am grateful for the respect I've earned, she wanted affirmation for her conclusion.

Evidently her surprised husband had heard our conversation and had praised her for the courage it took to do that, and was further amazed at the improvement in her outlook and attitude. They'd been in marital therapy for quite a while, with Wendy convinced that her husband was the one who needed to change to suit her. She (no surprise here) even found a therapist to side with her and tell her husband he needed to tap more into his feminine side to accommodate her needs and feelings. Hey—does that mean the therapist also told her to tap into her more masculine side to accommodate his needs and feelings? No, probably not. This marriage was going down the tubes.

*"You've opened my eyes and helped me to see the light and to me that gift is so special that I don't know how it could ever be repaid. The best part of this revelation is that my child will get to have a mother who can teach him how to live, love, and be the best human being that he can be. The ugly cycle that my mother left me as a legacy has been broken!"*

## Do I Have to Disconnect? Can't I Just Get Over It?

The pull most children have to be connected to a parent despite horrendous treatment is compelling—and awfully sad. It's like a magnetism that draws damaged people ever closer to more harm.

Dana called my program to ask me if it was wrong for her to not go to her half-sister's graduation from high school because her sister's dad would be there. It gets worse. The stepdad molested her, Dana's mother knew about it, and instead of throwing the stepdad out of the house, Dana was sent to Mexico to live with other family while Dana's mother kept her marriage intact. At least she sent Dana out of harm's way!

I asked her if she still had a relationship with her mother. She said, "Yes."

DR. LAURA: See, that I don't get. Your mother knew her husband was doing her ten-year-old daughter. She gets rid of her daughter so she can keep the man in her bed; you talk to her, but you don't want to talk to him; you don't want to go to the graduation because he is there, but you have no problem with her being there.

DANA: I've been wanting to cut my relationship with her.

DR. LAURA: She is evil, I hold her more culpable than even him!

DANA: I know, I know. My husband tells me that, and it's like a sick relationship.

DR. LAURA: But you know what? You keeping your mother in your life is just as sick as her keeping that man in her life. You are doing the same thing!

DANA: The main issue is like, I thought, okay, I'd get over it.

DR. LAURA: Frankly, my dear, "getting over it" would mean denial, and denial keeps you stuck and puts the rest of your family at risk.

DANA: She makes fun of me. She says, "Ah, you want to keep the baby away from us."

DR. LAURA: Your answer should be, "Yes! I do!" Of course you are not going to bring your family to her house. Of course you're not going to let your kids even know her! Of course you are not putting your children in harm's way with her husband! Of course not!

DANA: Okay.

DR. LAURA: Repeat after me: "I don't have a mother."

DANA: I've never had a mother.

DR. LAURA: That's right—and let me hear you say that again.

DANA: I've never, ever had a mother. Yeah, I know that.

DR. LAURA: Then start behaving as though you actually know what you say you know. Because what I hear from you is, "I know that, but I want my mommy to be different, and I want her to love me and protect me, and I want her to throw him out and choose me!" It's not going to happen. She is evil. She is not going to do any of that, Dana.

DANA: Okay. Well, I'm really glad I called you because it has been haunting me forever and ever. I've been wanting to get rid of them and say, "Okay, I'm not going to have any contact," but I want family.

DR. LAURA: You have a family.

DANA: I do?

DR. LAURA: Yes. You have a husband and his family, you have a child and friends. This all together is your family.

DANA: (crying) Okay, thank you very much.

An interesting thing happened at this point. I directed her to do some guided imagery. I asked her to tell me what she was looking at. "A wall," was her answer. I suggested that a magical door was going appear. When she could envision the door, I told her, "You're going to see your mother, your step-father, and some of these other folks who have given you a hard time. I just want you to see them all there, on the other side. They're not walking toward you, they are just standing behind that now open door. Tell me, Dana when you can see them all clearly."

DANA: Okay.

DR. LAURA: You want to name them off?

DANA: My mom, him, and my sisters . . . unfortunately.

DR. LAURA: Yes, unfortunately. I do agree with you it is unfortunate . . . it is what it is. Now, keep staring at that wall. What I want you to do now is to brick it over so it is no longer going to be a door—it's going to be an intact wall. Brick it over. No more door. Tell me when you're finished and take your time.

[Folks, you're just not going to believe what Dana says next!]

DANA: My husband is a bricklayer, and he is pretty fast.

[Can you believe that I guided her into an image that so closely followed her life?]

DR. LAURA: (laughing) That's great—let him help you! Tell me when you're done.

DANA: Okay, we're done.

DR. LAURA: It's six feet thick. They can't come back through it. I want you to turn around. Can you see your kid from where you are?

DANA: I can hear him.

DR. LAURA: Good enough. Can you see any of your husband's stuff?

DANA: Yep.

DR. LAURA: Okay . . . that's your family now and forever.

I asked Dana to call back the next day as a follow-up to what we'd done together. She told me that she realized that by backing off from her original family she's just trying to protect her current family. "So, I'm just very thankful because you took a one-hundred-pound weight off my back by helping me realize that I'm not that evil."

Can you believe that? Her stepfather molests her. Her mother abandons her. She's worried that SHE'S EVIL??!! That is just so typical of people damaged by a Bad Childhood because you naturally see yourself as the bad guy for resisting evil, defending yourselves, judging a parent negatively, and deciding to protect yourself and your family from them. Why? That position has a finality to it that eliminates hope. That's a bitter pill to swallow. Also, bad parents have probably blamed you so much that you doubt yourself. What feeds into that self-doubt (besides longing and guilt) is the intrusive actions of others who disagree with your perception and actions.

## When Others Disagree

Let me just say up front that simply because someone disagrees with your point of view or plan of action doesn't make you wrong! It is always worthwhile to take into consideration learned, insightful, wise, objective, caring input— just make sure it fits into most of those categories before you give it even a moment's attention! Frankly, most of the time advice and criticism are not objective at all, and are usually motivated more by the advice-giver's own guilt, hurt, fears, needs, anger, cynicism, or arrogance. I realize that you may be so stressed by your circumstances and feelings that it's hard for you to be discerning, but be careful about what you give weight and attention to.

Here's an example—very close to home. Pam called my radio program telling me that she disowned her biological mother because a cat is a better mother. Pam's mother was either drunk or hopped up on prescription pills, and perpetually running around on her dad. In fact, her mother took Pam and the other children to "visit" boyfriends while Dad was at work.

PAM: She didn't have to work. She had a house, cars, credit cards . . . she had it all. She started going to bars and she met someone else—so they divorced. We were taken into a home with a man who was an alcoholic, and um, he abused her, and she basically, emotionally abused us as well—and neglected us. I basically raised my two brothers and two half-sisters.

My father has been married now for twenty-seven years to a wonderful woman. The problem is that they do not understand that I don't want anything to do with my biological mother.

DR. LAURA: Whoa! What don't they understand?

[Here it comes . . .]

PAM: Well, they keep saying that my one brother doesn't talk to them. They had a falling-out and so they say they know what it feels like as parents not to have a child talk to you.

DR. LAURA: Are they aware of what she put you through?

PAM: Yeah, I've told them. They knew it was bad—but they didn't know how bad it was. I have explained it all to them. I've been in therapy for ten years.

DR. LAURA: What is your question for me?

PAM: I need to be able to say something to them so they will stop saying, "Well, she's still your mother; she gave you birth." Whoopy-ding for that! I just don't get it. I say to my dad, "You lived with the woman and you know what she's like."

DR. LAURA: I'll tell you, Pam, I believe I can explain to you why they are doing what they are doing. Guilt.

PAM: Guilt over what, though?

DR. LAURA: Guilt over what you and the other children had to go through.

PAM: Because they weren't there? Or they weren't as aggressive as they could have been to help us?

DR. LAURA: You are right on the money. Their guilt for not interceding is somewhat alleviated by their minimizing how bad it was. So if they minimize in their minds that it wasn't so bad, she is your mother, you should make contact, then they feel better. Your brother has broken off with them for some reason, and they feel guilt over that. How, then, can they justify your actions and not his? They can't. They're in a bind. What they are advising you is for their benefit, not yours.

PAM: Um-hmmm. Okay. I got it.

DR. LAURA: Here's the rule: when you clarify something to someone, and it's so blatantly clear that it is impossible for them to not "get it," it's because they can't and don't want to, because then they have to face something about themselves. So *you* have to understand that they don't want to feel some feeling—so they have to deny some of yours!

I can think of innumerable calls with the same issue. The "victim," actually, the conquerer, is being punished or criticized for extricating his or her life from a dangerous or destructive parent, while the motivation for that criticism is anything but benevolent. Mostly people are driven by self-interest, and generally people do not want confrontations.

Too many people will stand by and watch some form of abuse and not intervene because they don't want to be the next target or they don't want the stress or responsibility or they recognize themselves as either the perpetrator or the victim and just don't want to deal with it because denial is easier. The final category is ironically evil: it is the goody-two-shoes types who feel like such "good people" because they ostensibly will forgive anyone anything. In my opinion, this cavalier forgiveness rewards the evil and exploits the innocent one more time—all for the sake of so-called "goodness." Real goodness takes risks and stands between evil and the innocent, with courage of word and deed.

Irene, a listener, commented on the importance of setting boundaries in families by not allowing abusive family members back: *"My mother grew up with an alcoholic father. When my grandmother kicked him out of the house, my mother allowed him to move into ours. Unfortunately, not only did he bring in the chaos that accompanies an alcoholic, he was also a pedophile, which my mother knew, as he had abused her while she was growing up. He abused me as well. Years later, after I had completed therapy, I confronted my mother as to why she allowed him into our home. Her response was that she felt obligated to do so because he was her father."*

Irene's mother lied to her. Her motivations had absolutely nothing to do with obligation. Irene's mother derived a twisted sense of happiness being the one who forgave and took care of "Daddy." She was willing to sacrifice the well-being of her family and the innocence of her daughter all to become "Daddy's special girl," which is how she interpreted the sexual molestation by her dad. With this sleight-of-truth, she turned a heinous act into a good one so she could feel loved instead of facing what was bad. Now the abuse affected yet another generation because one woman refused to disconnect from a dangerous and destructive parent.

So when you're bombarded with friends and relatives telling you, "It doesn't matter how he/she treats/treated you, they're family, and that is all that matters," I believe you'll probably be justified in saying, "That would be true, if he/she hadn't torn up their parent card by _____."

Then inform them that they'd better confront their own demons, because without an honest assessment of themselves, they will likely pave a road to hell for others.

## The Kiss(-Off) Goodbye

Many people have written about how unburdened and relieved they felt to express fully what they went through as children, how it impacted them, the mistakes they made in dealing with those events, and what elements helped them eventually become a conqueror.

Many of these included letters sent to the offending parent. Melinda identified with a caller who complained about having a difficult time speaking directly to her father about the way things are and were. Her father had a problem with her not responding to him like one would expect a daughter would relate to a father. Small issue . . . she is thirty-six now, and he hasn't been in her life since he divorced her mother when she was six! I guess he thought that sperm DNA gave him rights and created emotional ties without the rest of him being around!

When Melinda heard my announcement about the preparation for this book, it got her thinking about her life, how she made it better, and how certain aspects of her past could repeat again in impacting her son. She knew she needed to address it and listening to my program gave her the "*kick in the behind*," as she wrote, to do so.

After she sent the following (excerpted) letter to her father, she felt as though she had finally let go of the pain that she had regarding her father and his life choices.

*Dear Walt:*

*This letter is to explain my reasoning for why I will no longer be welcoming you to be involved in my son's life. I cannot let you do to my son what you have done to me. You have been a great source of pain in my life. I have allowed you to hurt me simply because you are my biological father. When I was growing up, your conduct as a father to me was hurtful. You would show up to visit me unexpectedly and inconsistently, at times of your own choosing. When you left, I would sob for hours afterward wondering if the reason you did not visit me was because of something bad about me. You never sent me birthday cards. You never paid child support.*

*At first I thought this was about forgiveness. My husband encouraged me to have a relationship with you because he grew up without his father even knowing of his existence. He thought that at least knowing your father was better than not. I honored his request of being polite, and bit my tongue many times when I wanted to comment about the inconsiderate things you would say in my presence.*

*But over the years, I have learned it is not about forgiveness, it is about doing the right thing—which you never did by me. You had an affair. You slept with my babysitter. You never paid child support so we were on welfare. You threatened to kidnap me if Mom tried to get child support. You, however, always had a way of manipulating things to deflect away from your own lack of responsibility for me by turning the issue into one of greed. You turned things into you being the wronged one "because Mom and I were greedy and after your money."*

Melinda then challenged him to finally do the right thing by paying her mom back for all the years of back child support, taking complete responsibility for his own actions, expressing remorse, and making an effort to make things right and proper. She told him that he's always gotten away with what he's done, but that it stops here. She isn't going to pretend anymore that he is a "father," much less hers. In fact, she proclaimed her mother's second husband, her stepdad, her real dad, and her son's real grandpa because he walked the walk.

*This is no longer about me. I have my son's best interests to consider. For his sake, I cannot welcome you in his life. This is about stopping a pattern of being hurt by you.*

Finally, I am going to include in its entirety a letter written by one of my listeners, Violet, to her brother for the sake of her niece. Her brother is married with two daughters. Her brother also first had a child out of wedlock and pays little attention to her—which is all too typical. Violet believed that there is nothing she can do to mend the pain of a child's broken heart, especially when her own "father" has broken it. After being asked numerous times by her niece why her own daddy doesn't love her as much as the two daughters he had with his wife, Violet felt morally obligated to confront her brother. She's not sure that this letter struck any chord with her brother, but hoped that if I put it in this book, it would do so with someone.

I believe that Violet is wrong that there is little she can do to mend her niece's heart—this kind of solicitous intervention, and the love behind it, goes a long way to diminishing her niece's sense of worthlessness based upon her father's virtual abandonment.

The letter was written by Violet, but it was constructed as though the niece had written it. I am including it, in spite of its length, because I think it will say something important to all of you dear readers.

*Letter to My "Father"*

*It's been a while since I've wanted to tell you a few things, but only until now did I find the best way to do so. How long has it been since we last spent some time together? And how many things have changed since then, I couldn't begin to tell you. You know, sometimes I remember things we did, when we actually spent time together, things you probably don't even remember now. I fondly remember that winter afternoon, as we walked hand in hand along a path lined in leaves scattered all around. I'm not sure where it was, nor how old I was, it's been so many years that it seems almost an eternity has gone by. At least, that's how it feels to me. You probably don't remember, you've probably forgotten about it along with many other things. For better or worse, I remember; though nowadays, those memories are fading more and more, only leaving me with those old pictures we used to take.*

*Unfortunately, that which I remember the most about you, as I grew up and became a teenager, was your absence. Mostly, I fill the void with memories of things that never happened. Those chats at the dinner table that never happened; those words of advice I never got from you but so desperately needed; your jokes and anecdotes I never heard, and of course, the wisdom you never shared with me.*

*I wonder if you ever knew what I felt when I lost my first tooth, or how I would have loved to have your loving arms pick me up as my attempts at learning to ride a bike ended abruptly with my meeting the floor head on time and time again. I ask myself if you would have been proud of me for finally having learned to read on my own, or scored my first basket when I finally made the team. Come to think of it, you probably didn't even know I liked sports. It's sad to know that the man who gave me life knows nothing about me, about my dreams, my* fears, my successes, and my failures; and even sadder yet, that he never cared to find out.

There was so much I wanted to share with you, but I never found you, and you never looked for me. You know, I would've gladly accepted your reprimands right along with your compliments, because that would show me that you loved me, that you cared. You even deprived me of that.

Time has gone by, and the more time that goes by, the more I realize that I haven't lost you. I finally understand that I never had you. You should be proud of yourself, though, knowing that thanks to you, I've learned to survive and overcome many obstacles without you. Your absence makes me stronger. As time goes by, you're nothing more than a name on a birth certificate, which in reality means nothing.

I will no longer run to the phone with every ring, hoping it is you on the other end, wanting to know how I'm doing. I won't rush to the door full of hope every time someone walks in on my birthday, wishing it were you with a big, loving hug just for me.

To think that for such a long time, I tortured myself, trying to come up with an explanation or a reason as to why I was denied your love while my (half) sisters weren't. Was it that my mere existence was an inconvenience for you? I would ask myself why you treated me the way you did, why you would deny me the only thing I ever wanted from you: your love— something I thought was normal for a parent to feel toward their child. I've heard so many dads say their kids are a blessing. What about me, 'dad'? What am I to you? A mistake from your past, and nothing more?

I was very fortunate that God sent me an angel, and I have not grown up without a father. It's true, I grew up without you, but I now realize, I never lacked a true father. I had someone by *my side, who loved me as much and maybe more than I could have ever wished for you to love me; someone who made all my cuts and bruises better with hugs and kisses, and who cured my fevers with lots of love; someone who was there to rock me back to sleep on those nights when I had night terrors. That someone was not you.*

*I don't consider the lack of a father–daughter relationship between us a total waste. Without even trying, you taught me a great deal. From you I learned everything I don't want to be. Every day I thank God I'm not like you. Even at my young age, I understand the difference between you and me: I have a heart! I know what it's like to give your love to someone who brightens your existence. I've promised myself I won't turn into you. I WILL love my children.*

*Did I ever tell you I used to love you very much? Well, I did. If you didn't hear it before, it was probably because you never gave me the opportunity to tell you. I know I still have a lifetime ahead of me, but perhaps there won't be a future for you and me. Perhaps the next time you hear about me will be when you get my wedding invitation in the mail, or an announcement informing you that I've had my first child.*

*Keep in mind that if someday we do happen to run into each other, we won't be much more than strangers, no different than we are now. Our future is in your hands.*

*I only ask of you one last favor: give your daughters a hug and kiss on my behalf, one of the many that I once mistakenly thought I had a right to.*

I hope you noticed a number of things from reading this letter, probably through your tears. This letter is not hostile; it is frank, honest, sensitive, emotional but not hysterical, and leaves the door open without making promises. It clarifies the truth about her father's wrongs and the impact on her, yet makes clear her strength and commitment to a Good Life.

Even though this was written by the child's aunt, the child read it, approved it, and signed it. She owns it.

This kind of letter can be written even to a deceased parent. It is not the response that matters. It is your commitment to a Good Life through a healthy kiss-off.

SEVEN

# How Do I Get Love?

*At one point . . . my husband told me, "The only thing wrong with you is that your mom stole your childhood. She should have been loving you and she didn't. BUT, I AM going to love you and love you and love you until you get it; until you get it that I will always love you, no matter what."*

**—Amber, a listener**

Of course, the most obvious consequence of a Bad Childhood is a feeling of not being loved. Frankly, hurtful worry is at the core of most of your troubles in relating to others intimately, as well as undermining a sense of confidence in work, play, and life in general.

As I brought up earlier, it is surprising how many of you don't see the connection between your current attitudes and limitations and your childhoods. You know that you have "issues" about your childhoods, but you probably don't see that impacting your feelings, and don't recognize how your response to your childhood is largely determining your perspective and behaviors. Most of the time, this hurts your ability to feel and be loving in your life today.

A recent phone call from Simi to my radio program epitomizes this truth. She called and told me that she had a great husband and marriage, and an adorable four-year-old son and was a stay-at-home mom. Her problem? Well, just as things are going along fine, and with no warning, she will be consumed by what she called "anxiety." In response to this anxiety, she completely shuts down! She withdraws from all communication with friends, family, and her husband, and she completely stops taking care of all of her responsibilities around the house for the family.

I asked her to explain to me why she picked that particular manner in which to respond to the stressor of "anxiety."* All Simi would do is repeat herself.

I gave her a mini-lecture about fulfilling responsibilities and obligations despite such emotional upheavals and how doing so was elevating, while not doing so just added to her problems.

We were up against a commercial break, and so I asked her to think about what I said and ". . . to think about why you become a helpless child and make everyone take care of you." In those few seconds before the break she broke out with a huge, noisy, gasplike sound! I had just enough time to say, "Yes, there it is—think about that and I'll be right back."

When we came back from that seemingly endless, but only three-minute commercial break, I asked her about that gasp.

SIMI: I just didn't see the connection at all until you said it out loud. I didn't realize that I was becoming a helpless

---

*I highlight the term *anxiety* with quotation marks because people often name things to identify them to others, though the terms are not accurate representations of the experience—as you will soon see.

child wanting everyone to take care of me. It is so obvious to see now. My mother was very volatile, critical, and always angry. She always took her anger out on my siblings and myself when she'd come home and something hadn't been done to her liking. So, to avoid these outbursts, I TOOK CARE OF EVERYTHING! (she yelled)

DR. LAURA: So, Simi, it's not anxiety you feel, not really. You find yourself doing everything around the home for your son and husband, the resentment builds as though he—and your life in general—were your mother, you collapse, and then you don't have to do anything and everyone has to take care of you.

SIMI: Yes, that is exactly so. Oh my.

DR. LAURA: You want the "mother love" you never had. You are, as an adult, finding a way to be that child in your past to force your husband to be the source of your "mother love." There are two problems with this tactic: First, while your husband can "baby" you each time you collapse, he can't replace the forever-lost "mother love" that you yearn for. Second, each time you "collapse," your husband and son think less of you and you lose the status of who you've become.

Here is my suggestion for you, Simi: you need to ask as an *adult* for caretaking *appropriate* for you as an adult woman. When you ask for the caretaking appropriate to a helpless child, you have to become that child. When you ask for caretaking as an adult, you get what you really need now. So tonight, as soon as dinner is done and your son is in bed, put on something comfortable, grab the bottle of scented oil, and sweetly and seductively ask your husband to massage your feet . . . and . . . whatever.

Simi, DON'T LET YOUR PAIN AND DISAP-
POINTMENT OVER YOUR MOTHER'S NE-
GLECT ROB YOU OF YOUR JOB AS AN ADULT
WHO DERIVES PLEASURE AND SATISFACTION
FROM TAKING CARE OF YOUR FAMILY! *She* was
wrong to make you be the completely unappreciated, responsible adult when you were a child, but now *you* are
wrong to not appreciate the joys and blessings of being a
responsible adult.

SIMI: Oh, I completely get it. I feel so relieved and good
right now. I'm going to do just that tonight, Dr. Laura.
Thank you. Thank you.

I guess the student was ready to let me be the teacher.

The day before I began writing this chapter, I spoke with
a seventeen-year-old girl whose mother was now divorcing
for the second time. In this call I had the opportunity to
redirect a child's thinking before she became too weighted
down with ugly feelings about herself because of her
mother's inappropriate, unacceptable behaviors.

Since the latest divorce, Jessica's mother was quite promiscuous. Jessica was living with her mother and was been extremely upset by her mother's "slutting around." Recently,
Jessica, as nicely as she could muster up, told her mother her
opinion about her out-of-control behavior. Evidently, Jessica's
mother defensively retaliated for this criticism by telling her
she didn't love her and then throwing her out of the house.

Jessica moved in with her father, who fortunately is a nice
guy and a responsible dad. Nonetheless, when your mother
says she doesn't love you, not only does it hurt, it makes you
question your own value.

I explained to Jessica that it is hard to have objectivity

when criticized or rejected by a mother. Parents are the first natural source of feedback about you. When your father tells you that you're beautiful, your esteem soars and you feel beautiful; when your mother tells you that you are doing great at something, you enjoy doing that task all the more. As a child you are completely dependent upon your parents for both your physical and psycho-emotional well-being; your identity is formed, in large part, by how they see you.

When parents are negative about you, hurtful and destructive, it is very difficult for you to see them as being flawed and being mean. More typically, you take to heart what they say. After all, they are your parents and you can't really imagine that what they're telling you about you isn't true.

I told Jessica all of this and then described her mother as having "lost her last remaining marble," and said also that her mother was in "her 'jerk' phase." I explained that while her mother was in this jerk phase, nothing she said was to be taken to heart because it had nothing to do with Jessica, and everything to do with her own twisted inner world over which Jessica had no influence or control.

I reassured Jessica that someday, maybe not soon, but someday her mother would emerge from her jerk phase and would be available as a loving mother. However, until that time, she was not to imagine for a moment that any of her mother's hostile, hurtful behavior had anything whatsoever to do with her at all.

DR. LAURA: Bottom line, Jessica, I don't want to hear that you started fooling around with boys, drinking, trying drugs, and doing other self-destructive behaviors because you're upset that your mother doesn't love you. You need to look at her with *objectivity;* that means to pretend you are from Mars, observing her and drawing conclusions about her actions. When you do that, from the position of a Martian and not her daughter, you can clearly see she is way off track and what she says isn't about truth, it's all about her own messed-up mind right now.

JESSICA: (laughing) Yes, I guess that's right.

DR. LAURA: Good. That's the difference between objectivity and subjectivity. With objectivity you, the Martian, are looking at her wondering what's wrong with her; with subjectivity you, the needy, hurt child, are looking at her wondering what's wrong with you.

JESSICA: Yeah, that makes sense. Oh, and I'm not the kind of kid who would do all those bad things. My father is great and I'm happy here.

Gaining that sense of Martianlike objectivity, that that which your parents have done to you is about their bad self and not yours, will be your saving grace. Elizabeth wrote to me about coming to that realization. *"I am fifty years old and have had a very stressful, hard life. My mother is now seventy-five years old and in the final stages of Alzheimer's. I hate to admit it, I feel sorry for her, but can't say that I have any other feelings for her. She beat me all through my childhood and I married at nineteen just to get away from her. I struggled for years with self-esteem issues.*

*"After my second and last child was born, I went into counseling and took parenting classes. I spent most of the time trying to come to terms with why my mother hated me so much. Just recently, I concluded that the beatings had nothing to do with me."*

What a freeing revelation!

*"I am very happy to say that the abuse cycle stopped with me. I knew what not to do as a mother. I hugged them a lot and made sure that they knew that I loved them. They received a lot of positive*

*reinforcement. I am proud to say that both my son and daughter are able to tell me anything and ask me anything without fear of judgment . . . we reach mutual resolutions."*

I believe that one of the reasons some of you, abused as children, become abusive adults (toward yourself, your spouse, and/or your children) is because you haven't become objective about your parents' behavior; you took in their treatment as the measure of youself and have punished yourself for being presumably inadequate or unlovable. Consequently, you have become so angry, unhappy, and defensive that you take those negative passions out on others in order to deny or relieve yourself of your emotional pain.

(Please read this last sentence five times before moving on with this chapter.)

You have to stand back and say out loud, "My mother/father is a jerk! It is not and it never was about me! He/she is a jerk and I am not wasting any more time, energy, and emotion diving off that platform again!"

(Please repeat the last two sentences at least five times before moving on with this chapter.)

What is the next step? The next step is making the *decision*, literally *choosing* to have a Good Life in spite of how bad you feel about yourself. Too many of you have come to believe that you can't have a Good Life until you learn to love yourself. My opinion is that this concept, while incredibly popular, is totally wrong.

I took a call from a woman who asked me how she could learn to love herself. She imagined that without self-love, she wouldn't be able, and shouldn't be expected, to do loving, healthy things for anyone, including herself. She said she was obsessed with this concept.

I told her that I have never opened my eyes even one

single morning of my life giving any thought whatsoever to if or how much I loved myself and that I couldn't imagine ever doing so. She was quite argumentative. I persisted. "My dear, our value, our lovability, does not come from some private emotional assessment—it comes as a product of our actions toward others. Contemplating our own navel is not the way we gain self-respect, it is by contemplating our place in the lives of others."

As you might expect, there was a tremendous response to my position, as the more popular position about *self*-esteem is quite self-oriented.

Tamey wrote a witty letter in response to hearing this call: *"I'm listening on your website streamlink (*www.drlaura.com*) to a caller from yesterday who is worrying about 'loving herself.' Your response was so right on.*

*"It occurs to me that she is afflicted with an illness common to many, many people in this life: SELFISHNESS, bless her little heart (my Mama always maintained that you could say anything without offense as long as you follow it with a comma and 'bless her little heart').*

*"Dang, that girl needs to get a life! For pity sakes, foster a child! Learn CPR. Be a Big Sister/Brother. Challenge yourself! Go downtown and talk a pregnant teen into giving her baby up for adoption. Adopt one yourself if you're good Mommy material. Throw out your TV! Learn to quilt! Learn how to cook! Cook a meal for your parents, your friends, a co-worker! For crying out loud, mow the lawn! Do something!!*

*"I could get hysterical imagining myself getting up in the morning, trying to decide if I LIKE myself!!*

*"When I get up in the morning (I usually try NOT to look in the mirror—way scary) I am so busy wondering about a million things: Did I take out something for supper? . . . Is anyone going to*

miss the bus? . . . *Eggs or pancakes? Naaah, cereal—I made pancakes AND eggs before church Sunday . . . PBJ or can we splurge the $2.50 for hot? Maybe the little kids, the kidlets, won't notice if they get PBJ and I let the midlets have hot lunch since it is much more cool . . . Should I ask him now about the lighter I found in his pocket or delay the war? . . . Is it too late for an abortion at fifteen? Oh, yeah, we don't believe in that, duh! . . . Ok, forget the red sexy one, if I cut out ALL sugar from now until spring break can I fit ANY swimsuit under size 16? . . . Since last night didn't work out with a fevered baby in our bed, could he possibly go for a hot lunch date in the Bronco? I could wear the black DK sweater—that sucker shows some cleavage! . . . Why is that child in the corner and when did I send him there? . . . Please God, I hope it was this morning and not last night!* "Get up to the table and eat honey . . . yes, I know you're sorry, we'll discuss the consequences after school . . . try not to worry." *Surely I'll remember what he did by then!*

"I don't even have time to write this fax. Kids are off, laundry and dishes going, I'm dreaming of writing another chapter in my novel, sucking on a celery stick while I pay bills.

"A moment, friends, to ponder . . . DO I LIKE MY-SELF????? (crunch, crunch . . . shrug). I have no clue, honey; and heck, I may not even deserve it, but I sure am happy!"

How is it possible that she could be so happy when she doesn't even know if she likes herself, much less loves herself? How is it possible that she could be so happy when she's seemingly got so much stress going on in her life? How is it possible that she could be so happy when she's not even sure she's doing everything perfectly enough that she could like herself?

The answer is easy: because she's not living for herself. I've reminded you several times now that happiness does not come from what you *get*, it comes flowing from what you *give*.

No human being is worthy or lovable in a vacuum. This notion of you having unconditional love from yourself or from others is a myth, a fiction, an impossibility. Your worth and lovability are products of what you give, not just that you breathe.

Christine, a listener, wrote to tell me that she had intended to call my show the very day she ended up only writing to me. She was going to complain about her *self*-image. She wrote that she felt ugly inside and out. Instead of calling, she tried to imagine what I would say. She figured that I'd probably ask her about what she was doing with the sixty pounds she'd put on during the last four years. She was pleased with herself for losing fifteen of them in the last several months.

Then she imagined that I would ask what she was doing to make her inside beautiful . . . and it struck her right then that she was doing NOTHING. *"No service, no giving, no loving, no nothing. For the past four years I've closed myself off to everyone but my husband. My poor children have had a shell of a mother. This was painfully brought home to me when my oldest daughter heard me saying that my children were a joy to me. She laughed and shook her head as though I were being sarcastic or making some kind of joke. I felt so bad about that, that she would doubt that I find joy in her very existence. What have I done to the children?"*

With that twinge of conscience, she started to contemplate, and with that came two images to her mind: first, she thought about Eleanor Roosevelt and Mother Teresa—who were not classically beautiful people, but people of such beautiful spirit because of their actions and loving service; second, she tried to think of the last time she had given love like that to serve somebody besides herself, and could only think of one woman from another country whose husband had abandoned her. Even so, she had not stayed in touch.

She had rarely opened her heart to another living soul. *"I have isolated and strangled myself. I have rebuffed people who have tried to be friends. As I realized all this, I also realized that everything that could make me beautiful is in my control. It will take effort on my part to correct my bad behavior by becoming more loving of others, and open myself up to all the love there is for the taking. I am so sorry that I have been so turned inward and focused on myself, when I could have spent these years helping others to feel good instead."*

Having had a Bad Childhood will certainly make you attentive to your wounds, vigilant to more prospective wound-makers in your life, somewhat leery of the possibility of a Good Life, and determined to get reparations for your pain. Since all of these are *self*-focused concerns, they counter efforts for a Good Life—for a good life is about an exhalation, not an inhalation.

Which brings me to a call with Tina, a human vacuum cleaner, or an extreme case of inhalation. Tina is thirty-two, and said she was embarrassed to let me know that she always has been insecure and jealous (the latter generally follows the former). She is in a now seven-year relationship, without shacking up, and has an eleven-year-old daughter. She told me that because of her insecurities, she feels like she's not showing any love.

TINA: I'm always telling my daughter, "I know you don't love me, and I hate it . . . and I don't know what to do."

Frankly, I went kinda, sorta ballistic in my head and heart. The thought of her driving her daughter crazy by being an unloving, ungiving parent and then making it worse by constantly challenging her daughter's feelings for her, wanting reassurance from the very creature she's supposed to be giving it to, made me see red. What kept me from going over the edge was that she at least knew it was wrong. That fact made the situation hopeful.

DR. LAURA: It is not true that you "don't know what to do." What you're really saying is that you're too uncomfortable, too scared, too needy, too self-centered to change. If you say that you don't know what to do, then no one can expect you to change, right? Ignorance, while not bliss, is your excuse. First thing you have to do is stop abusing your daughter. This is psychological abuse.

TINA: Yes, I agree.

DR. LAURA: I want you to close your eyes and repeat out loud, "I am going to give to my daughter, not take." Let me hear it.

TINA: (crying) I'm going to give to my daughter, not take.

DR. LAURA: That's right. Now just sit with that. Right now, I don't think you understand how good that is going to be for you. Right now, your whole life is geared toward you getting what you never got. And you know what? You're never going to be totally filled up . . . that's just the way life is. But what you can do is *become* more loving. Instead of becoming a vacuum cleaner, trying to get love from everywhere in the world, you are going to be a water fountain, spraying love everywhere.

At this point, we argued back and forth a bit as Tina resisted the notion of giving up her lifelong quest to have everyone, even her child, constantly reassure her and love her in spite of her selfish behavior. So as I have done with many callers, I led her on a guided imagery journey to help her see and, believe it or not, feel the difference in her life and heart when she shifts from a taker to a giver.

I asked her to close her eyes and picture in her mind, without telling me the details, the kinds of things she does to her daughter, friends, and boyfriend when she's in vacuum-cleaner mode.

TINA: Oh my God! (makes pained-sounding noises)

DR. LAURA: All right, stop! Open your eyes, shake your body.

TINA: (crying deeply)

DR. LAURA: That was pretty upsetting, wasn't it?

TINA: Yes . . . she doesn't deserve it.

DR. LAURA: Shhhhhhhhh. Close your eyes again. Okay, now picture the things you will be doing differently as a water fountain.

TINA: Ohhhhhhhhhhh.

DR. LAURA: Isn't it nice?

TINA: (sounding upbeat) Yeah.

DR. LAURA: Don't you feel good? Don't you feel happier?

TINA: Yes. But I don't know how.

DR. LAURA: Of course you do—you just did it in your mind.

TINA: You're right, I did!

I told her to give her daughter kisses, hugs, and compliments, rub her back, and brush her hair into a ponytail. Amazingly, the next thing out of Tina's mouth was that "I was always told that I was ugly." Here we ago, "me" again!

DR. LAURA: Well, maybe you are, and who cares? Your daughter doesn't love you because you are pretty or ugly.

Your daughter loves you because you're Mommy. It doesn't matter how pretty you are unless you're entering a beauty contest next week. You are back to thinking like a vacuum cleaner. That will happen; change is neither immediate or without glitches. Keep working on being a water fountain—and believe me, Tina, when people are thirsty, they don't much care how lovely the fountain is, do they? Call me back in a week.

She didn't call back. I hope that doesn't mean she shifted totally back into being a vacuum cleaner. Besides, millions of others heard that call, and hopefully they found direction from the experience.

Jeff is one of the listeners who responded to that call: *"I'm listening to your show right now . . . and earlier you had a caller on who just didn't know 'how to be happy.'*

*"Then, later on, you had a gentleman on with terminal stomach cancer.*

*"I find it amazing how people who have no health problems, financial problems, etc., find things to be unhappy about . . . when other people in the world are dealing with terminal stomach cancer and other illness outside of their control.*

*"It's time for some people to wake up, start being grateful for what they have, and stop whining and complaining . . . and making up reasons to be unhappy. Life is too short to do this.*

*"I know—I've been there before . . . and your show has been a wake-up call. I'm choosing to be grateful and happy every day I'm alive."*

Many of you might have been made angry by Jeff's letter, protesting that he doesn't know your pain and he can't possibly understand what you've been through. Fair enough. But my thought has long been, what difference does it make how you got into the hole or what the hole is lined with—there's only one means of getting out of that hole: choosing to be grateful and happy every day you're alive.

A young man, twenty-four years old, called my program recently, complaining that the man he thought was his dad wasn't.

DR. LAURA: You mean, some other guy knocked up your mother and took off, and this man, whom you've always assumed is your dad, raised you?

JOE: Yeah.

DR. LAURA: And?

JOE: I feel betrayed—and as though my whole life has been a lie.

[Here we go—a self-induced Bad Childhood moment!]

DR. LAURA: You're mad at the man who raised you?

JOE: Yeah. They should have told me the truth. I feel betrayed. He's not my dad!

DR. LAURA: Joe—what are you thinking? Some guy knocks up your mother and evaporates—you're not mad at him and you don't feel he betrayed you. Some guy steps up to the plate, marries your mom, and raises you as though you were his own flesh and blood—and you're mad at him and feel he betrayed you? Are you nuts? Is your life so boring that you have to troll for pain?

JOE: Oh. I never looked at it that way.

That's my point: much of our suffering is based on "how we look at things" (negative attitude) and "what we don't look at" (the beauty and possibilities in life). No one, certainly not me, is denying the reality of abuse of many kinds, and the impact the damage done has on your ability to see and embrace the positive. Nonetheless, there is only one way out of that hole, and that is by letting the beauty of life in, and using your life to add to it.

One caller in particular, Don, epitomized this image of embracing the dark rather than the light. He called because his girlfriend had died the previous Saturday night of an overdose—perhaps an "unintentional" suicide. His parents were both dead and he had no friends—obviously by his own making. He had no one to talk to, so he called my radio program.

The reason he had no friends, he told me, was that he didn't like people because he couldn't trust them. What he had in common with his girlfriend was that dark, negative attitude about life and people.

DR. LAURA: Did she have a negative attitude about life, too?

DON: Yes.

DR. LAURA: Shame.

DON: Yeah.

DR. LAURA: Have you thought about suicide?

DON: Yes.

DR. LAURA: What do you think about people who are happy, and have family and friends? How is it possible? How is it possible that some people trust and like others and have a pleasant life, taking children to the zoo, and all?

DON: I guess they feel good about themselves . . . I don't know.

DR. LAURA: Why would they feel good about themselves? I'm sure they've all been through some crap in their lives, just like you have. Why do they feel good about themselves? And is that a requirement for having family and friends?

DON: I'm not sure.

DR. LAURA: Is it possible that many people can be trusted—and that you're wrong about that?

DON: Yeah, I could be wrong.

DR. LAURA: Your girlfriend found one way to deal with the negative view of life. You have the opportunity to find a different way—to join with people who are happy—most of the time—nobody's happy all of the time and not everybody can be trusted.

DON: Yeah, that's true.

DR. LAURA: But a lot of people can be trusted, and that's why some people are happy—because they are willing to find out which ones can be trusted. You've just decided to eliminate the whole human race . . . and that's why you think of suicide . . . but do you really think that your girlfriend had the better idea?

DON: Killing herself?

DR. LAURA: Yeah, killing herself; was that a good idea?

DON: No—because she said she loved me.

DR. LAURA: Maybe she thought she couldn't trust you. Maybe she had that same negative view. See what happens with negativity? It grows into more negativity until it becomes hopelessness. This is an opportunity for a turning point for you. You can embrace life now that you've seen what the alternative brings—she has no more chance to be happy.

I asked Don to take me back to some time he can remember in his past when he was happy. He picked having a cat named Calico when he was a child. When I asked him what about that cat made him feel happy, he talked about unconditional love—with no strings.

I countered with, "That's not love. It's bonded dependency. There is no unconditional love in the universe, except from God, but other than that . . . we have to contribute to our own savings accounts—they don't grow without our input." He felt he had input for this girlfriend, but didn't quite know what to do to help her with her hatred for herself.

DR. LAURA: She hated herself? Why?
DON: Because her family hated her. Her dad raped her.
DR. LAURA: That's ugly. But you were there to love her and be her friend. She pushed you and everyone else away to embrace the ugly.
DON: Yep.

Having picked up on his desire to help her, I suggested then that he perhaps get involved in helping someone who would embrace what he had to offer. I suggested he go back into AA and possibly become a sponsor or help some underprivileged kid with a sport—turns out Don's good at golf.

DR. LAURA: Instead of wallowing in the crap, how 'bout you try to make some other people happy by virtue of what you have to offer? And Don, you don't have to feel happy to do it—you don't have to be perfect to do it—you don't have to feel totally loved, valued, valid, and valuable—you don't have to feel any of that whole package before you can go out and do something of value. You clearly have it in your heart to help people—let that part of your heart go free.

To another female caller, Nina, who wanted people in her life, including her children, to know about her molestation as a child, so that they would "understand and know her better," I said (brace yourself), "Who you are is what you've built, not what your stepfather and whoever else did to your genitals! Telling everyone about your dark past is to elevate yourself on a pedestal of victimhood, which you probably hope makes everyone bow to your desires, moods, and feelings, and will permit you a range of self-centered demands, and excuse you from responsibilities as an adult, a woman, a wife, and a mother!"

I'm sure some listeners took umbrage at that advice. One listener, Nancy, wrote that I was "cold and unprofessional," and that I had a "Get over it!" attitude. She went on to describe the pain and problems that she and her sister have experienced since their molestations by their father. She rightly talked about how the abuse means more than even the sexual acts, where everything in the relationship is "viewed through that screen." She accused me of minimizing the devastating impact sexual abuse has on so many areas of a child's development.

I disagree with absolutely nothing Nancy wrote clarifying the horror and destruction of parental abuse, sexual or otherwise. Nonetheless, I take the risk of being misinterpreted whenever I try to move people past their histories, no matter how despicable the acts perpetrated on them. Influencing you to move on and not define and limit yourself by your Bad Childhood is not the same as telling you to "get over it!" You will never, ever entirely "get over" your Bad Childhood. My point is that you have to find a way to put the past in some place other than your lap in order to move on to a Good Life.

Another listener, A.M., also wrote about her response to that call: *"I too had a miserable, rotten childhood that included abuse, but I have all of those stories firmly packed away in a box and I let the weight of my blessings keep the lid on it."*

This is poetic and a much better mentality than holding historical painful memories tight to your chest—too close to your heart.

Friends, YOU *ARE NOT* WHAT HAS BEEN DONE TO YOU. You *are*, instead, who you choose to do for and with others today.

If you don't get that message, you will never find peace and happiness, and instead you will likely play "head games" for most of, if not all of, your life.

One caller was doing just that. She called my radio program, ostensibly with the concern that she takes out her insecurities on her husband. What are those "insecurities?"

Trust, she offered, and a fear of being hurt.

I started with the fact that all human beings take a risk when they decide to trust, and all human beings who take such risks find themselves dealing with hurt at some point in the relationship—even when it is a good one! I reminded her that there were no special exceptions or exemptions from that simple truth of life.

She was not going to give up or into any such philosophizing. She determinedly went on, declaring that she realized it was *her* problem and she knew she was being annoyingly unkind and driving herself nuts.

Okay—I went with it and asked her seemingly standard questions about how they met, and so forth. You're not going to believe this: "He has been unfaithful to every woman he has ever been with. BUT I KNOW FOR A FACT THAT IT'S DIFFERENT WITH ME!"

If that last statement doesn't drop you in your tracks, I don't know what would.

"So, you have trust issues and are afraid to be hurt, so you team up with someone who has proven beyond a shadow of a doubt that he can't be trusted—but you know for a fact that he's trustworthy with you, which is why you continue to have trust issues? Neat package, woman."

Here's the setup that explains this head game she's playing with herself: She is afraid to be vulnerable because of her Bad Childhood. She never learned to believe in the sincerity and compassion of love, since she has been hurt for trying. Her psychological defense mechanism is to keep a distance. Her human need is for closeness and companionship. She marries a guy for closeness, but one who can't be trusted, validating her lifelong behavior of keeping a distance, and also giving her a darn good reason not to grow and change.

There is possibly another twist. If this guy actually does not have an affair, then she will have redeemed what she thinks is her own bad self—the combination of her "low self-esteem from childhood" and her outrageously annoying current behavior. Put another way, her husband is a guy who can't/shouldn't be trusted; if he comes through for her, then she is "special," and she's really loved, something she never got to feel with her parents.

No matter how it works out, she is filled with her past and that is not a constructive way to live in today, especially with a two-and-one-half-year-old daughter who is experiencing constant Mommy-hysteria in the house.

My final, albeit mutually unsatisfying, advice was to choke herself into behaving more positively for the sake of her child, from whom I did not want to hear in fifteen years with Part 2 of this story: *her* Bad Childhood.

This and other types of head games are all about trying to keep *control*. What you couldn't control in your Bad Childhood you control in your adulthood, thinking it will lead you to a Good Life. Wrong!

Amber, a listener, was very excited hearing about my work on this book. She wrote that she almost laughed out loud because I seemed to be talking about the themes of her life. Her mother was a teenage runaway and her father a gang member who picked her up on the streets of East L.A. in the late 1960s. She never knew her violent "sperm donor" (vs. actual father) because her mother took off with her. After a failed marriage, her mother married for six years, at which time Amber learned that her stepdad was not her dad. After that Mom got into the party lifestyle in the drug culture of the 1970s: drugs, alcohol, pornography, and random sex.

"*What I struggled with the most was the men in and out of the house and her bed. I hated hearing it. I hated seeing it. I hated . . . smelling it. She'd sleep with men for money, for approval, for thrills. Sometimes I would sleep in her bed when she was out, hoping that I could prevent her from bringing another one home. On those nights they would simply go into my bed. Later I would have to wash my soiled sheets along with clothing I would find in them. This was my introduction to sex and intimacy. I felt absolutely desperate, alone and afraid.*"

Her mother continued to spiral out of control with drugs, alcohol, and rage. She was very unstable, and often physically abused Amber. Sometimes Amber's mother would come into her room and say, "I just feel like beating you up." She told her she couldn't wait to be rid of her. During her junior year of high school, she came home to a house wrecked and mostly empty—her mother had split. "*I was relieved that I wouldn't be beaten that night. I felt a little bit safer in the house. Nonetheless, I felt angry at her selfishness and, ironically, I felt abandoned as well."*

Though she had been disgusted by her mother's behaviors her whole life, she began to go down the same road, experimenting with drugs, alcohol, and sex. *"These were reckless and dark years. Life was just getting from one day to the next. I didn't eat much and was sick a lot. All I cared about was partying and trying to find fulfillment and acceptance in meaningless relationships. I tried to fill myself with these things—that just left me feeling empty, miserable, and racked with guilt and shame."*

When she was in college, her life changed. She went to church and, following Christian concepts of moral choices and actions, found peace, forgiveness of herself for her out-of-control behaviors, and an enormous sense of gratitude for *"this miracle of life."*

However, her problems weren't over. Here is where the issue of control comes in. As a result of her childhood experiences and growing up under the influence of the feminist movement in the 1970s and 1980s, she had little respect or appreciation for men. Since she felt she could never really trust anyone to take care of her growing up, she became overly self-sufficient. It served her well in getting herself through college, but it didn't contribute much of a positive nature to her marriage at twenty-four.

Once married, she determined to be in charge of everything: she wanted to control, and in her mind she was the only one who would do things correctly. She always complained when things were not done her way.

Seven years later, she grew tired of being constantly vigilant and negative. That was about the time she started listening to my program. *"By following the advice on your radio program, I slowly learned to surrender control. Even now, the words feel sooooo good! Surrender the need to control! Luckily, I married a TERRIFIC guy. No exaggeration, he is a gentle, kind, faithful, honest, loving MAN. So, my learning to surrender the need to control him was only made difficult by my background and my stubbornness.*

"*Needless to say, with time and effort, I am a changed woman—blissfully happy and madly in love. But this process had further ramifications that I could not predict. Since I could so tangibly see results in myself—my feelings toward my husband and his behavior toward me—that tangible realization helped me to release the need to hold onto my past as well.*"

Amber ended her lovely letter by telling me that she was grateful that God granted us all free will, because she is FREE to CHOOSE her life rather than be burdened with continuing the cycle of abuse or using the past as an excuse for weak behavior.

By the way, Amber is an at-home mom, homeschooling her two boys, and is in the process of adopting abused and neglected children. How beautiful, fulfilling, and full of love is that? Clearly, Amber learned that spending one's whole life trying to grab onto a better yesterday provides few benevolent tomorrows. Opening your heart, taking the risks, and confronting the hurts and disappointments even the best Good Life contains, will bring peace and love.

"Mind games" and "controlling" are not the only "focused-on-yesterday" techniques people hold onto so dearly, wondering why they can't find love. "Perfectionism" is a typical technique of trying to get over yesterday while destroying today.

Rebecca, a listener, wrote to me of her struggles with perfectionism as a result of her Bad Childhood. She wrote, "*I often hear callers tell you how they were abused as children and don't know how to be happy as adults.*" She wanted to share her experience, strength, and hope with others by contributing to this book. She was hoping that she would be helping others to become as happy as she is today, after eighteen miserable years of living in an abusive household.

Her father verbally and physically abused everyone in the family. Her mother would stand by and do nothing but whimper while the kids were all being beaten, hit, choked, and even stabbed. Her brother turned heavily into the drug world. Rebecca turned into Little Miss Perfect, trying to save her brother and keep her dad from getting angry and her mother from getting even more sad.

When she turned eighteen, she couldn't take the family abuse, secrets, and sickness anymore. At one point, she convinced her mother to leave with her. That didn't last long; predictably, Mom went back to her dad. Rebecca met a guy and "fell in love." Unfortunately, he was too close in personality and behavior to her father.

*"I was so miserable trying to say the 'right thing' to get him to stop and love me. Sound familiar? My unhappiness, feelings of unworthiness, of not being pretty, smart, funny, wild, or classy enough, etc., is what I learned from Al-Anon, what came from living in the family with alcoholism."*

The underlying thought process for Rebecca, and so many others with a Bad Childhood, is that if they were good enough at "whatever," they could fix those around them, and live in peace and love. You look constantly toward fixing others and are frustrated by your failure, which further lowers your self-esteem.

*"My whole life, I never had to look at myself. I spent all of my life focusing on what other people did or did not do, didn't say, thought, didn't think, etc. I used to spend a lot of time and energy worrying about yesterday and tomorrow; today, I live in TODAY."*

The core issue with perfectionism is the tyranny that comes from it. Rebecca, for example, would find herself yelling and causing scenes with a salesperson in a department store if she felt a feeling anywhere close to the one she felt at home with her parents. She would blame other people when situations didn't go her way because she couldn't bear to think of herself as other than perfect; if she did, then her whole abusive life would have been, in her incorrect thinking, her fault!

With the help of Al-Anon, she has adjusted her attitude about perfection, accepting and adjusting to the realities of today on today's terms. Consequently, she is able to be dating a healthy, decent man with whom she hopes to someday build a good family.

Ruth was a caller in December 2004. I remember giving her a difficult time, telling her that demanding perfectionism from her children was a form of child abuse. Wow! Talk about dropping a bomb! Of course, these calls all start the same way, with the caller focusing in on their own feelings and needs for love, all the while seemingly blind to what that obsession will mean to those near and supposedly dear to them.

Ruth would rationalize and justify being tough with her kids, making them conform to her expectations and demands, by saying, "It is in their own best interests. I'm doing it for them." WRONG. She was doing it for the sake of her original, dysfunctional family! Here's the way it goes: if you could be perfect, then your parents would be happy and you would be loved. That didn't work, so the next step is making your kids be perfect, all to accomplish the same impossible goal. That becomes cruelty. The bottom line is that all those around you have to feed your damaged ego or you sink into the despair of your childhood. When they don't reflect back your desperately required picture of yourself, you either get mean or depressed, or both.

Believe it or not, I had a heck of a time even getting her to admit that she'd had a Bad Childhood. Like many of you, she was living her life in total response to it, but in serious denial about it. She just didn't want to admit to and look at the truth of her life. If she did, there would be a lot of pain to contend with that she's been avoiding, as well as the necessity to be objective about what she's doing to loved ones today.

The same day we spoke on my radio program, she wrote me the following note:

> *Thank you for your time today. I called you this afternoon to ask how I can overcome my need to please and look "perfect" to everyone. It became apparent that my real issue was how I have been mothering my children.*
>
> *I have been pondering our conversation for an hour, and I want you to know that I get it. Yes, I did have mean parents, and yes, perhaps I am a little damaged. But, I now realize that I have control over my own actions. I may not have control over my feelings, but I choose at each moment what to do and what to say.*
>
> *The abuse from my parents as a child may indeed make me prone to feel a certain way or to want to lash out and criticize my children, but nothing they have ever done or will ever do can take away my control over my actions. When I am mean to my children it is because I am choosing to be mean. And it is time for me to make some new and better choices.*
>
> *Thank you for helping me realize my own power, as well as my limitations. I hope that with time and maturity, my feelings about myself and about my children will improve. But until*

*then, I will DO THE RIGHT THING regardless of how I feel.*

Jolene called my program wondering if she were so damaged with her upbringing and the things she's gone through that she's just unable to love and be loved. She believes that her current husband and she are both so needy that neither one of them can get fed.

DR. LAURA: Do you like cookies or candy better?

JOLENE: (laughs) Oh, cookies!

DR. LAURA: If I give you a million cookies and you actually have to eat a million cookies, are you actually going to enjoy that?

JOLENE: No.

DR. LAURA: If you eat, say, two cookies and wrap the others up and start giving them to people, and they say, "Ooh, aah, thanks," do you think you'll enjoy that more?

JOLENE: Giving the cookies *away* after I've eaten mine?

DR. LAURA: That's the problem with hungry people—they think the only way they're going to feel good is to eat. That would probably be so if you were a guppy, but human beings tend to get more satisfaction out of giving. So when we spend our time saying, "I'm hungry, therefore I just have to keep gorging myself . . ."

JOLENE: That's true. And I'm so afraid to—to express how I feel for him because I'm not even sure of that. I'm afraid that then I'll be the doormat that he can walk all over because he's gonna have some power over me.

[This is the core issue for all of you who express fear of giving: that the only result of vulnerability is hurt, the kind of hurt you experienced as a child.]

DR. LAURA: And then what's going to happen? What's the worst thing that could happen after you've been hurt? You die?

JOLENE: No. I would be alone or would not have anyone care about me.

DR. LAURA: How is that different from how you are living now?

JOLENE: It's not. That's true. I never even thought of it that way.

It is jarring, isn't it, to realize that what you've been avoiding all along is exactly what you've created out of your fear and avoidance? Wow!

What's the next step? To behave AS IF you believed in love, kindness, faithfulness, serenity, safety, intimacy . . . and so forth. In other words, you choose to behave counter to how you feel, realizing that this means being trusting, giving, and flexible.

Trust is a decision, not a mood, and it doesn't come with a guarantee.

Giving is a loving act, not attached to any demands.

Flexibility is about survival.

Notice I don't talk about a *change in feelings* as a first step. I am quite often misunderstood with respect to my position on "feelings." I find myself being described as someone who doesn't believe in feelings (heard that on the TV program *20/20* one time), or hear callers say to me, "Oh, I know you don't like feelings." This confusion is a product of my insistence that you behave properly in spite of your feelings. I will often push a caller to tell me about facts, responsibilities, and decent behavior by saying, "I didn't ask you about your/their feelings, I asked you about what was actually said, or what actually happened, or what you think a mature, responsible person ought to do."

If you wait for some special feeling to come upon you that will automatically unleash comfort with complete trust, forget it. If you focus in on *your* feelings in the context of all your important relationships, you'll never get what you need. If you can't bend with current realities because you are still rigidly defending against the threats of your early life, you'll always break.

Here are some useful, hopefully inspiring quotes from listeners on the subject of feelings motivating behaviors:

- *"I struggled with fear of being alone, fear of losing everything, fear of no one loving me and a terrible lack of trust in myself. I struggled with shame on my marriages failing and so many other things.*

  *"I am learning to keep my behavior positive and appropriate and behave myself through life. I am learning not to let feelings guide me, but to let good behavior guide me. I redefined what my purpose in life is, and I decided to be a role model for my daughter."*

- *"My advice to anyone still struggling with a chaotic or horrible life is to know that it can be different. Even if you can't feel it yet, believe it and start to act accordingly. Your radio show was a daily support to me, my three hour pep-talk and guidance counselor. Your book,* How Could You Do That?! *was on my nightstand for a year as I read and reread the different sections. This was the time in my life when I started thinking about doing 'the right thing,' and not just the easy thing or the feel good thing. I put my son first and I slowly started to adopt more moral behavior. This was not an easy change in some ways, but as I started to make the changes and the chaos of my life began to subside into a more rich and substantial peace, I went from tip-toeing down the road to running full speed. Why didn't anyone tell me how wonderful life could be? Doing the right thing isn't deprivation—it's the most wonderful reward!"*

- *"I stopped going to Adult Child of Alcoholics meetings after a while because I found them too concentrated on 'the problem,' and I wanted my life to be about 'the solution.' I still struggle with looking at the good, not the bad in life. I also struggle with the need to be perfect or nothing. I have finally begun to understand that you do not need to feel better before you behave better. As you have often said, Dr. Laura, feelings follow appropriate behavior."*

- *"I had to struggle with bad thoughts about myself, from what I was directly and indirectly told as a child, and my attitude about men being the enemy thanks to my mother's bad choices and many mates. My behavior reflected my attitudes, and as a result, I had a hard time trusting people, mainly men. I also struggled with self-inflicted fears: of being alone, a failure, and never having a healthy relationship because I perceived myself as damaged goods.*

    *"I just woke up one day tired of feeling worthless, looked into my precious daughter's eyes, and told myself that I WAS A VALUABLE PERSON; to my daughter first, therefore to myself. I realized that if I wanted to be valuable, I had to behave valuable, for my daughter's sake and for my soul's sake."*

If a Good Life is your goal, then the means to that end have to be accepted: YOU have to reach out; YOU have to take the risks; YOU have to face life's natural bumps in the road with more equanimity; YOU have to stop interpreting everything uncomfortable or unpleasant in terms of your

Bad Childhood, instead of simply the cost of living life; YOU have to stop taking out your fears and hurts on others; YOU have to let yourself enjoy the blessings in life; YOU have to accept that neither you, nor others, nor life can or will be perfect; YOU have to be willing to join in with all humanity as we search for peace, love, and purpose.

So, my friends, the answer to the question asked in the title of this chapter, "How do I get love?," should be clear: *be loving*—nothing fills you up more.

EIGHT

# The Good Journey

*What happened happened. It is too easy to wallow in self-pity. I decided to become better than the monster and win the battle. Much of what happened to me is not my fault. How I handle it is my responsibility.*

**—Teresa, a listener**

*It was a long hard journey that has been worth it to get through. . . . I have a wonderful, fulfilling life that I am so grateful for.*

**—Leah, a listener**

*I am now 31 years old, and though sometimes I still struggle with my inner thoughts and feelings of failure and self-hatred, I know that I have a choice in how I behave. It is very easy for me to fall into my old ways of negativity and nastiness, but I know that if I act "as if," things will be so much more wonderful.*

**—an anonymous listener**

The Good Journey from victim to conqueror is not a slide on ice, and it does not take you to some magical place of pure, stressless happiness. The Good Journey is asymptotic, which is a mathematical term for a curve that continuously approaches but never quite arrives at a destination free from horrible memories and their resultant current challenges.

Please don't let those two facts of life dishearten you; being up to your waist in the warm, gentle surf on a sunny day with a cool breeze is still an incredible experience, in spite of the ebb and flow of tides and currents, the inevitability of intermittent clouds, rain, and high winds, and the temporary discomfort of high and low temperatures.

In other words, the Good Journey is less like a complete cure, and more like a daily challenge in dealing with the symptoms to make sure the "disease of your past" no longer infects your whole life. If you choose, and it ultimately is a choice, not to take that Good Journey, your life becomes a broken record.

A recent caller to my radio program demonstrated what kind of life comes from this broken record syndrome. Karen is forty-seven years old, newly divorced and complaining about having become a "horrible procrastinator," and is now having her adult daughter take care of all of her affairs.

DR. LAURA: Since when?

KAREN: Um, ah, it—it's just been—I would say, the past, well . . . probably since my divorce (sighs), which was about ten years ago.

DR. LAURA: So you don't take care of yourself—and [big leap here] you're constantly waiting for someone to take care of you—and it's just not happening?

KAREN: I was married to someone who was gone most of the time and I'm the one who did all the finances, cleaning and took care of the kids—I managed everything. He would be gone for three or six months at a time. So I-I-I guess after my divorce I-I pretty I-I-I just stopped . . . caring.

DR. LAURA: My guess is that you've been waiting your whole life for someone to take care of you. Which makes it seem counterproductive to marry someone who not only doesn't take care of you—but is rarely even around! Sounds to me like an avoidance of the very thing you say you want, but are too uncomfortable to have and too afraid to ultimately lose. I would imagine that you got competent at caretaking yourself at a very young age. So you did what you knew—you married your parents. Take me back to when you were seven years old and tell me what's going on in your house.

KAREN: (laughs) Seven years old, wow. We were pretty much left on our own, you kow. My mom and dad were busy. My dad worked evenings so I never saw him. And my mom was just busy taking care of all the kids. And there was not a lot of personal attention.

DR. LAURA: And then you married a guy to keep that story going. And you still ache to get the attention. However, now you are decompensating and abdicating all your grown-up skills and responsibilities as a last-ditch attempt to get someone to take care of you. You're still emotionally hungry from age seven.

KAREN: I'm very stuck.

DR. LAURA: You are stuck in your old pain.

KAREN: Well, isn't that kind of silly at forty-seven to feel that way?

DR. LAURA: Silly, no. Sad, yes.

I asked her to think about all of this for about two days and then to call me back. She had a lot to deal with and to see in a different light. She did call me back, sounding much more energetic and positive. She admitted to having found it quite difficult to comprehend the concept that she still wanted her mom and dad to take care of her, but she decided to do a lot of thinking and she started writing down her thoughts. At that point, feelings and ideas just came flowing out of her.

KAREN: The four most important points that I came up with thinking about myself at age seven were . . . I didn't feel connected to my parents or any of my siblings. We were all four years apart—and those are big years when you're young. I felt my parents were very unapproachable. I just couldn't go to them with a problem or talk to them about anything. And I pretty much felt like I had to be invisible or else I would be getting into trouble. I wanted to be the good girl, so if I were invisible and quiet and not having to have somebody notice me, then I was a good girl.

But I think the most important thing is that there was some traumatic things that happened to me as a child that I felt my parents should have stood up for me or fought for me—there's a little resentment about that.

[Just when you thought the skies were becoming completely clear . . . ]

But I don't know how that ties in with still wanting them to take care of me at forty-seven.

DR. LAURA: You don't? Procrastinating about your basic responsibilities in life is designed to *force* your daughter, your friends, and whoever to take care of you like a parent normally takes care of a helpless, dependent child. At forty-seven you are making everyone you can be your mommy.

KAREN: But I understand that that's never gonna happen.

DR. LAURA: Yes, I know you understand that. But emotionally you don't want to give up.

I then gave her a mini-lecture on *giving* as the key to *getting*. I explained that her whole life is focused in on what she didn't get and what she wants now in order to make up for what she didn't get . . . and that's why she has bad relationships. Everyone she deals with *today* is dealt with only within her personal context of a wanting *yesterday*. I told her that the only cure to her dilemma is giving. I asked her to think about that overnight and call me the next day.

She called back and, boy oh boy, did she ever get it!

KAREN: Yesterday you said that the only cure you know for me was by giving. And you wanted me to think about that and get back to you. So, after much reflection, I've come to the point, and I don't know if I'm on the right track here, when you say "giving," maybe you mean, um, giving the things that I've been hiding from people the most like trust, caring, and thinking about others before myself.

[HALLELUJAH!!!]

Because the void that I had, missing from my mom and dad, is about being needy, which is about taking. The opposite of that would be giving and maybe that would fill the void.

The second part of that is that I realize that by procrastinating I'm thinking, "Who is it hurting except me?" I'm the one getting myself in trouble here, getting deeper in trouble, and I realized that it's a very selfish act. I mean, a lot of people are affected by my procrastinating—like all the people I owe. So, it's a very selfish act. And I never thought of myself as a selfish person.

DR. LAURA: Because you were absorbed in holding onto the hope of being nurtured as a child by a parent.

KAREN: Yeah, and you also had asked me when it started? I told you ten years ago after the divorce. But after thinking about it—I've always procrastinated. It just got worse after the divorce. I need to make some big changes—I've been like this my whole life. Think by building up those walls which I know I have—I don't let people in—those walls are solid, and . . .

DR. LAURA: That's your fear of not being nurtured at war with your need to be nurtured. "I'm gonna procrastinate, be helpless and all of that so people will take care of me—on the other hand, I'll be damned if I let them close because I don't want to be disappointed again." That is a living hell.

I suggested that in less than a week she move from hell to purgatory, and that the only place to go from here was heaven!

Another caller, a twenty-five-year-old woman, married and with a two-year-old daughter, wanted to know if she should, as many friends and relatives supposedly suggested, write a book about her bad childhood as a way of alleviating all her pains. On the surface, that may not seem like a particularly unusual thought or question. However, and interestingly, in spite of the fact that she was on hold for over half an hour waiting to come on my program, when I greeted her, she was "all choked up" and crying through her words. Frankly, I didn't believe the tears.

At first the caller attributed some physical handicaps to her mother's drinking. While I indicated I was not a medical doctor, I did say I was unaware that the syndromes she men-

When I was in training as a marriage, family, and child therapist, I had a client who would sit through each session crying her heart out, and her sinuses too! She would work through an entire box of Kleenex during each appointment. She would pile the used tissues up on her lap and not throw them away until after the session was over.

After several weeks of this, I reported to my supervisor that I was perhaps not suited to this profession since I felt no sympathy for what was clearly her constant display of pain. He asked me if I'd found myself so unmoved with all the people I was working with. "No," I replied, "just her." He explained that I wasn't resonating with her "pain" because there probably wasn't any!

After giving that some thought, I risked seeming totally cold and without compassion, and asked her in the very next session, "Every week you pile up used tissues on your lap—to what are they a monument?" At first she looked at me as though I had just smacked her. At that second I felt sickened—but then the crying stopped and the real talk and work began.

Not all crying is about sadness—many times it's about manipulating others, bringing attention to one's self, soliciting caretaking, controlling others, ducking criticism, and so forth. I believe I'm reasonably intuitive at discerning between real pain and those motivations.

I believed this caller was creating one of those moments.

tioned were tied into maternal drinking—and that she might be stretching a bit in making her mother responsible for some of her physical challenges. I asked her if she thought she had fetal alcohol syndrome. She said no.

I asked her if writing a life story at twenty-five, outlining her pains due to her mother's behaviors, wasn't a bit premature, since she didn't have much understanding of the middle and the end of the story! I also wondered aloud if she would be including all her inappropriate and hurtful behaviors, whether to self or others, that might be a product of her internal struggles and defenses. This is where the discussion went south.

She became angry with the focus being off her mother and onto herself. So what did I do? I pushed harder, reminding her that she has a wonderful man who loves her and is committed to her in spite of her physical maladies, and she has a little girl who looks up to her as a goddess. "You know," I continued, "I think you have two choices: one is to be your mother's damaged, hurting child; the other is to be your husband's wonderful wife and your daughter's loving mother. I think you have to pick one, because a focus on the former, in my opinion, distracts you from the latter, and makes you feel entitled to things that make their lives with you inappropriately compromised."

At this point she decided that I didn't know what I was talking about, I was completely wrong, and I could not possibly know anything in a few minutes on a radio program.

Nonetheless, these two scenarios are apt examples of what happens when you don't take the Good Journey: your life becomes dedicated to your Bad Childhood.

Dr. Jean Beninato, a dentist in Massachusetts and a good friend of mine, forwarded me this e-mail of unknown (at least to us) authorship. I think it makes a great segue into talking about the choices and options for your Good Journey:

> A young woman went to her mother and complained about her hard life. She was tired of the struggle, felt like giving up, but was willing to hear advice from her mother.
>
> Her mother took her into the kitchen, filled three pots with water, and added carrots to one pot, an egg to another pot, and coffee beans to the third. She turned the heat under them up to HIGH and let them boil.
>
> At the end of about half an hour, she removed the carrots, egg, and coffee beans from the pots and put them on plates. She asked her daughter what she saw and learned. The daughter had no clue. So the mother explained that each of those three foodstuffs had been exposed to the same challenge: boiling water. The carrots went in strong and sturdy and then turned to mush. The egg went in fragile and ultimately turned hard. And the coffee beans changed the hot water around them—producing a wonderful aroma and a delight to the taste buds.
>
> "So, my darling daughter, when the hour is the darkest and the trials are the greatest, how do you handle adversity? Are you a carrot that loses its strength? Are you the egg that becomes tough and hardened? Are you the coffee bean that influences the universe in a positive, hopeful way?"

You could ask yourselves the same questions with respect to the Good Journey. Without your commitment to your journey, you will continue to either be quivering, ever-suffering mush, or self-protective, distant, tough and bitter. You choose.

*"Many believe that children can get through these things* (abuse and neglect), wrote Wendy, a listener. *"We can, but not without scarring. I now live a full and complete life that I think is the best revenge. I do however still suffer from nightmares, fear things that normal people do not and I still struggle to feel happy. My sister suffers the same. Children who suffer as my sister and I did, never truly get over what they endured. I believe that I will always remain haunted by my childhood.*

*"In contrast to the statistics of victims of abuse, my sister and I are both happily married with children. We even both did it in the right order with loving and caring men."*

Even those triumphant coffee beans, once boiled, will show the wear of their ordeal—they may become a bit puckered and bleached. But they still create something to share with the universe: aroma and flavor. The Good Journey is not perfect, but it is good.

*"No one wants to think about the terrible things that adults can do to children. I certainly don't. So it's not difficult to imagine my surprise when I learned my own mother was a survivor of the worst kind of abuse,"* wrote Bilinda, a listener. She told me the most remarkable story about how she learned of the physical, sexual, and emotional abuse her mother and aunts and uncles suffered from at their own father's hand with their mother, Bilinda's grandmother, just standing by.

The more she learned about her mom's childhood, the more she was thoroughly amazed at the wonderful woman who was her mother! *"I learned that at some point, after the despair she felt that led to an attempted suicide, she made a decision to live and make a difference. I am living testimony of the difference she has made. She has given me a legacy of faith and sacrificing, uncon-ditional love that I will pass down to my own children. Her choice gave me life."*

I am always in awe of people who choose to climb out of the deep holes others put them in and contribute nothing but beauty and love. It is not too late for you to do the same.

Vanessa wrote about being nervous about motherhood. She is completely aware that up to this point in her life she has done everything destructive to her own body and life to avoid becoming her worst fear: her abusive mother!

Then she made a choice, to live the life she probably would have had she not intersected with her abusive "mother." This is what I call taking the proper course. In sailboat racing, my hobby, there are innumerable hard-to-remember (and some-times hard-to-understand) rules. One of them states that under certain circumstances, you cannot sail your boat in such a way as to "mess up" another boat you're competing with. You are supposed to sail your proper course, meaning what you would do if no other boats are present. We call this "sailing your own race." Well, I would suggest you choose to live your own life.

Vanessa has educated herself on the mechanics of good parenting. She married a man whom she brags has all the makings of father of the year. They are dedicated to making certain that she will be home with her children. These are all the right choices . . . so what happens to the fear?

*"The rest I will do afraid . . . until the fear is gone. I'm fairly certain that once I am pregnant, the excitement will overwhelm the fear and I will find myself head over heels in love. To others, I would advise: once your childhood is over, you are responsible for what you become. A bad childhood may explain aspects of your personality or character, but should never excuse choices that you make.*

*"There is no joy in remaining in the war-torn ruins. Get up and*

236 Dr. Laura Schlessinger

*find out what it is that you were put here to do—then, do it!"*

Too many of the people with a Bad Childhood who wrote to me had to reach a horrible bottom before they made the *choice* to take the Good Journey. They were, sadly, like Deborah, who wrote, *"When I was twenty-six (thirteen years ago) I sought counseling. I was in a desperate place. I was suicidal, deeply depressed. Although counseling was not the cure for me (I felt they perpetuated problems and keep you in therapy rather than help you move on), I did have an epiphany one day. That epiphany was that I had had a miserable life for twenty-six years, but that I could change the next twenty-six years of my life.*

*"It finally dawned on me that I could make choices which would affect my future. Up to that point, I took no responsibility for my choices and felt like I would never amount to anything. I won't say that I suddenly and miraculously changed, but my life is very different now. Slowly I began to succeed in my life. I felt healed and valued by my control over my own life."*

I am hoping that this book will help many of you avoid getting to the point of self-annihilation. There is a way out of, or improving, every situation you find yourself in; and those things that can't be fixed can be endured, learned from, improved—and never repeated.

How do you start this Good Journey of good choices? While there isn't one narrow, specific "to do" list, many listeners shared how they went about it and brought up a number of appropriate concepts, concerns, and advice.


## 1. Writing a Journal

You may get a tremendous amount of insight into yourself from writing in a journal (tape-recording is another technique) while you are consumed and driven by "whatever" emotions, and then read and evaluate your words and thoughts later when you are more calm and objective. In doing so you can learn a lot about your immediate emotional (over)reactions and (mis)interpretations of the words and actions of others. Furthermore, you can discern which of your thoughts and actions were appropriate to the circumstances, and which were obviously right out of the past and not appropriate, useful, realistic, or constructive in the here and now.

Don't use a journal-writing experience to just whine about your past and present woes, complain about the thoughtlessness and sensitivity of others, or document the "righteousness" of your sadness. Instead, use the idea of a journal to help you "therapize" yourself, to tap into the wisdom and awareness you have within you, in spite of what you feel is utter emotional or psychological chaos within your being. You are deeper than that.

## 2. Historical Perspective

As I've said, going over your Bad Childhood story again and again only solidifies your negativity and "victim" mentality. However, looking at your past for what was wrong *and* what was right is an effective way to get perspective—and perspective brings positive feelings and increased peace, believe it or not. This is by no means a whitewash—remember, denial is yet another mechanism of staying stuck. This is instead an opportunity for you to sift through to the "Oreo cookie in the compost heap," and there always is one, metaphorically speaking, of course.

Make going over your past a study of what you have

learned, not just about what you have suffered. This is the perspective that is beneficial. This subtle change of focus brings a picture of what you have become versus what you've endured.

The next step is to look for what, if anything, there was in your Bad Childhood that helped you ultimately become as healthy and functioning as you are! For example, in order to survive a parent who was hypercritical and demanding, perhaps you've learned self-discipline; to survive a parent who was negligent concerning your basic caretaking, perhaps you learned a degree of self-sufficiency that serves you well today. It could be that you've overdone the degree of the "self" part of discipline and sufficiency (compulsive if not manic)—that can be tempered, of course, but the main bonus is that you have those positive traits.

Ultimately, it is your strengths that will pull you through. Feed them so that they will have the strength to overcome your weaknesses.

### 3. Self-Evaluation

It is so easy to complain about your past and blame it for your behaviors, neither of which give you power to make anything be different in the rest of your life, nor to bring joy into your life. Looking in a $100\times$ magnification mirror at your enlarged pores, scars, lines, wrinkles, and other imperfections is not what any of you will likely line up to do! Nonetheless, evaluating your character traits, your strengths, and your weaknesses gives you a jumping-off point for personal growth.

What you're good at, celebrate and nurture. What you're not good at, admit to and search for role models and help to repair or change. Don't worry so much about people thinking less of you; when you ask them for help they will see you as brave—at least, the decent people will.

### 4. Pick Your Human Environment

Be more in charge of the people you surround yourself with and invest yourself in. Choose groups and individuals who will help you be and do your best, not wallow in negativity. Only hang around people who for the most part—nobody's perfect—live the kind of life to which you aspire. Surround yourself with good people, even if they are not your family. Avoid bad influences like the bubonic plague.

Please recognize that the so-called *guilt* you think you feel for marginalizing dangerous and destructive people and circumstances from your life isn't guilt at all; it is fear and/or longing. The fear refers to your concern about more punishment and hurt if you don't conform to their demands. The longing—well, that's obvious—everyone wishes for the basics of a healthy, loving, and happy family. Sorry.

### 5. Choose to Be Good

Every minute of every day of your life you make choices in the expressions on your face, the words from your lips, even in your body language, which also communicate your inner thoughts and feelings. Every minute of every day of your life you also make moral and ethical choices, which also communicate your inner thoughts, feelings, and character. Try to really spend time being aware of what you are being in the lives of everyone you interact with, from your teacher to the store clerk to the guy who puts gas in your car.

Your life is not just all about you—it is about everyone you now touch.

Remember that everything you do to other people impacts their day and their inner world the same way it does for you. Your Bad Childhood, as I've explained earlier, traps you into a mode of thinking only about yourself and how you feel. The quickest way out of that corridor is thinking about your impact on others.

If you have developed destructive habits or attitudes as a result of coping with your Bad Childhood, only you have the power to fix them. This will probably be the biggest struggle you'll have because habits hover right under our immediate awareness. If someone reasonable comes to you to constructively criticize some way you habitually behave, don't strike them down and don't run and hide. It took guts on their part to approach you, and they clearly want to help you be better. Don't counter with, "Well, you're not perfect, either." Instead, stay put and listen with humility. In fact, take notes, because it will be emotionally difficult to hear with appropriate objectivity.

Plan ahead to notice those times when you reflexively cry, yell, hit, break, run, and so forth, and figure out in advance some other response. Of course, it will feel awkward to you and you will feel frighteningly vulnerable . . . but remember, before bread can be buttered, the batter has to be kneaded, rolled, punched, and put in a very hot oven.

If you think you're unsure of what road to travel, project yourself ten years in your own future with the opportunity to guide yourself today . . . what choice will make you proud? That's your answer.

## 6. Give Others the Benefit of the Doubt

It is just too easy to assume that every possible unpleasant or critical look or comment is a throwback to your Bad Childhood and an instant replay of the abuse and negativity that enveloped you. That makes it difficult for you to give the benefit of the doubt when it is due—and even when it's not. The pure act of *not assuming* ill will is a relief, is probably statistically correct, and gives the other person wiggle room to correct their position.

If you give that benefit of the doubt and find out that it wasn't due, that's fine too. You were decent and they weren't. The difference is clear, and then you can decide what your response is going to be with that person now and forever.

## 7. Disable Your Replay Button

I'm amazed sometimes at how so many callers with any level of Bad Childhood seemingly yearn to relive their historical pain in great, gruesome detail by explaining it all to me, as they've clearly done so many times before with anyone who would listen. When I try to stop them from recalling and retelling their stories, I can tell that I am frustrating them and making them angry. Believe me when I tell you that it is not out of a lack of compassion that I stop them—quite the contrary. It is because I have great compassion for their inability to move on in their lives that I try to disable their replay buttons.

The more you repeat that history in your mind, in a "therapy" group, or with anyone who will listen, the more you make your whole being about that, and only that. The more we go over the same path, the deeper the track we create—until it becomes almost impossible to veer any way out.

## 8. Embrace Values, Morals, Ethics, and Religion

I know that sometimes I express dismay and disbelief when callers don't seem to know right from wrong. I sometimes have to work hard not to sound condescending when confronted with, "Should I let my parents, who physically beat all us kids, take my children overnight, because after all, they are the grandparents?" It seems to me that this would have a simple, slam-dunk, obvious, no-argument kind of answer. I'm so often stunned that this is even a question!

I force myself to remember and realize that this is obvious to me because I did not have the absurd reality they grew up with. The norm for me is a home in which right and wrong were lived and taught. If your home has one or two parents who are virtually moral and civil criminals, then this was clearly not the case for you. So right and wrong may not be so obvious to you. Also, your drive to be loved and stay connected to horrendous parent-types leads you to ignore moral issues completely if they got in the way of that desired but insidious bond.

How can you now learn about morals, values, and ethics? You can learn them from watching others you respect, reading books, attending classes and lectures, listening to the Dr. Laura Schlessinger program (couldn't resist that one), and going to a church, temple, or synagogue, making sure that they are "traditional" in their approach, relying on scriptures versus political correctness.

Perhaps not surprisingly, in the thousands of letters I received in preparation of this book, the overwhelming majority named God and religion as their biggest saving grace; next came some relative, friend, or eventual spouse who believed in them.

The common thread through the thousands of stories about divine intervention and connectedness is a feeling of being loved in spite of experiences or misbehaviors, a recognition of support from decent people, and a format or blueprint for creating a better life.

## 9. Tolerating the Discomfort

I have told many a caller frustrated with "getting better" that they had to learn to endure, to tolerate the discomfort . . . a little bit longer. That is my version of AA's "one day at a time." It is a major struggle to break down the way you have lived your life, change the beliefs you have had, and rebuild it differently. Perhaps it seems to you like adding insult to injury: you are the one injured, and you are the one who has to change?! Yikes!

But that is the truth. The bad news is that it is difficult; the good news is that your life is now in your hands, not the hands of those from your Bad Childhood.

What is it exactly that you have to "endure?" You must tolerate the discomfort of giving up everything "familiar," and you'll remember that I already said that you will tend to gravitate toward the familiar, no matter how damaging, threatening, destructive, or dangerous—simply because there is a distorted sense of comfort in what you know and think you understand and believe you have under some sort of control.

Clearly, your relationships with destructive people will have to change dramatically or end completely. Of course, there will be resistance on their part, which will be a combination of threatening and seductive. You have to endure those feelings of wanting to reconnect.

You will also have to endure changing your own behaviors with almost everybody significant in your life once you realize that many of your actions were *reactions* to your own private pain and fears, and are not necessarily appropriate to today.

## 10. Gunfight at the OK Corral?

I have stated time and again with great emphasis that I don't believe in the healing power of confrontations. Confrontations were psychotherapeutically popular from the 1960s, when all authority was disrespected; this gave permission for young, liberal psychotherapists to use their patients to further their own political/psychological agenda by having them attack their authority figures: their parents. It was open season on parents. I remember scores of people coming to me for therapeutic intervention when I was in private practice as a marriage and family therapist, frustrated and confused, but not better off, from having had such a supposedly "purging, cathartic experience" that would bring "closure to their pain." Instead, it mostly left them isolated from their bio-families when such a disconnection was not necessary, unsatisfied that nothing constructive came out of it, feeling guilt for the havoc they had wreaked, and lost as to where to go next. Clearly, confrontation was and is not a panacea.

No, my friends, shootouts at the O.K. Corral session aren't the way to peace and serenity.

However, *facing up* to that parent's continued behavior is important, because it means that you are strong enough, in spite of yesterday, to deal with today in a self-respecting, strong, appropriate, grown-up, righteous manner—as an adult in your own right, and not simply as their frightened, dependent, weak child.

Peace comes with a price. If you're not willing to pay it, you won't have it. *Facing up* implies that *you* take responsibility for what you are doing to your life now. *Confrontations* imply that *they* take responsibility for what you are doing to your life now. I hope it is obvious to you which has more power to make your life better.

## 11. Compassionate Benevolence

This is probably one of the most difficult concepts of this book. The idea here is to assess your family member's place in the *annoying–evil* continuum, and then, once you decide they are on the annoying end, to change your behavior toward them from angry and resistant to understanding and compassionate.

You might find that minimizing contact, not letting them provoke you into fights or triangulating you into family disputes, is difficult at first, but practice makes perfect. Having absolutely no contact is sometimes necessary in situations where a family member is exceedingly dangerous or destructive to you and your family. But most of the time, when your family is somewhere on the annoying—not evil—side, you might find it more emotionally comfortable to make that once-a-month visit or phone call to check in or participate in a level of family dynamics that is acceptable.

Having some modified contact and controlled communication requires a lot from you:

- a growing level of self-confidence, as your ego becomes less dependent upon their behaviors
- an acceptance of the limitations of who they are and what they have to offer
- making a truce in your own mind about the past (which is not the same as forgiveness)
- a concerted effort to not take their dysfunctional actions and words personally
- a decision that "something," no matter how limited, is better than "nothing"
- the development of a healthy outside life, filled with wonderful people and activities to minimize your desperation for a fantasy happy ending with your family

## 12. Living for Something Outside Yourself

All of you who wrote to me about your Good Journey said the same thing: that without this journey, your total life's focus is on YOU, your victimhood, pain, disappointments, difficulties, and so forth. The main road sign pointing to the Good Journey is a focus on what you mean to or can do for others. For many of you, stuck as you are in your bad habits and constrained by your fears, this is a most difficult enterprise. Yet it is the most rewarding aspect of anyone's life.

Being *giving* to children, spouses, friends, neighbors, and strangers through charitable activities is *the* way you bring peace and happiness to your life, not by grabbing and maneuvering to *get*.

Real happiness is a product of the fulfillment of your obligations and responsibilities to others; anything is simply called "fun."

## 13. Emotions Are Not Truth

All listeners to my radio program, at one time or another, have heard me admonish a caller who responds to my request for facts by saying, "Well, I *felt* . . ." with, "I didn't ask you how you felt—I asked you to tell me what was said/done, etc." Feelings have become such a central part of our society's approach to life and problems that rational thought, values, and laws have become pushed into the background and everything is considered only by virtue of how it makes you feel—as though feelings had an IQ or were a directive.

Imagine for a moment, if you can, that you are an amoeba. Now, an amoeba does not have a complex nervous system and brain comparable to a human—in fact, it doesn't have a brain at all. When an amoeba finds itself up against some noxious chemical or a sharp object, it simply moves away in a direction away from the threat. Humans with complex brains, up against a threat, often first go through feelings before taking action. The feelings could range from disappointment, to frustration, fear, abandonment, or vulnerability, all based on earlier life experiences. Meanwhile, dealing with the threat of the moment in some concrete way becomes secondary to marinating in all these old, familiar emotions.

I have to wrestle people every day on my program about their absolute reverence for feelings: if they *feel* that someone doesn't like them, betrayed them, meant to "get them," isn't showing proper regard and respect, and so forth, they are committed to behaving as though it were true. This mentality results in more fights, bitterness, and unnecessary pain than life actually calls for.

Here's what you need to do: when you feel a strong feeling, ask yourself how much today is involved in it, and how much of your yesterday; then be willing to confirm whether your emotion is accurate. This means you have to be willing to communicate, ask the question, get the facts, dig for understanding, and be open to truth. You are best to start this communication from a "benefit of the doubt" point of view. If your worst fears are confirmed, *then* you can go to war! If your worst fears are not confirmed, you lost little time in bringing serenity into your life.

## In Conclusion

You can have a Good Life no matter how Bad your Childhood. It may not be a perfect life. You may never have all aspects of your life filled with serenity or the level of success that might have been yours had you picked different parents (just kidding). While some of you may never, for example, choose to have children because your anxieties about parent-childhood problems overwhelm you, you might feel comfortable volunteering in a preemie ward, where they always need loving folks to comfort children.

Your profound fears of intimacy may preclude you from becoming close to one person, so you might give of yourself by participating in civic programs, religious missions, and so forth.

It might just be that engaging in activities and relationships that are more comfortable, related to but not quite the ultimate goal, still may eventually get you there—slowly, indirectly, but surely. Or, it may not. Admittedly, not everything can be overcome. But just like that amoeba I mentioned earlier, you, too, can move away from danger and hurt toward some compromise position, even if at this point it is only in your own mind. That compromise position is still progress, and still superior to an all-or-none mentality.

You have to define for yourself what a Good Life means. Most of you will agree, I hope, that a Good Life has to do with what you do, what you mean to others, how you handle life's normal challenges, and how much you appreciate your blessings and opportunities. A Good Life is not about feeling good all the time. A fireman rushing into a burning building to save a child is not feeling good about it . . . he's scared and worried for that child, his family, and his very life. Nonetheless, he runs in because a Good Life comes from meaning something, not having everything.

Be the fireman.

# Postscript

Upon hitting the SAVE prompt on my computer after finishing the last line of this book, I became choked up. That's never happened after completing any of my previous eight adult books. What makes this book so special? Three things. (1) I was deeply moved by the courage and character displayed by people who have suffered significant pain at the hands of others they should have been able to trust and count on. These are people who realized and were willing to face and change the mess they may have created for themselves with counterproductive thoughts and actions that were a reaction to their Bad Childhoods. (2) I felt that this is probably the most important book I've ever written, based on how much I believe it is going to help change people's lives dramatically for the better. (3) Finally, I realized that I could not have written this book any earlier in my life because I had to be well down the road of my own Good Journey, and I was pleased to be able to see myself in that context.

Both of my parents are now deceased. While I will share

some of my personal issues with you, I am not anonymous, as are all the contributors to this book, and I don't wish to do damage to my parents, even after their deaths. Therefore, this will be more philosophical than autobiographical.

About one year before my father's rapid course of stomach cancer took his life in the weeks following his diagnosis, I remember him commenting on the huge number of people who came to the funeral of the wife of one of his coworkers: "Gee, I wonder how many people would come to my funeral?" It was an unusually candid moment for my father, and I believe it was probably one of the few introspective moments of his life. Perhaps he had regrets at that time for not having nurtured relationships. He was a very difficult, compulsive, critical, and argumentative guy—though he could also be very charming.

The last day he was coherent, I asked him the question of my lifetime: "Do you love me and have you ever been proud of what I've done with my life?" I remember the moment, thinking that his answer would change a lifetime of anguish and instantly transform me into a more peaceful and happy person.

He looked at me calmly and simply said, "Yes."

Obviously, that was the answer any daughter would want to hear. I waited, as one does for the thunder after the lightning strikes, for something magical to happen to me. I should have been happy or satisfied or something. Absolutely nothing happened. I excused myself and walked out into the back yard and paced around his pool. I was trying to figure out why I was not moved. The realization came to me quickly. My father had always been tough on me, so tough that during one spring break week in college, I actually stayed in the dorm and survived on a bag of Oreo cookies rather than come home to his browbeatings. Nonetheless, it has been clear to me for a long while that my drive to excel was directly related to a desire to finally please my dad. I can look at his impact on me as both positive—I worked extremely hard to do something of value—and negative—I found it extremely difficult to enjoy my successes.

By the time of this last conversation with him, I had pulled back the lens and was looking at him with objectivity. I was not the little girl trying to get approval from her dad. I was a grown, competent woman looking at a man who had been petty, insensitive, mean, thoughtless, demeaning, and down-right unloving, all for the sake of his own ego. He'd been a jerk, I suddenly understood, so naturally what he had to say really didn't, and shouldn't, matter. Believe me when I tell you that was a stunner. To think that much of what was not healthy about my life was a reaction to him—wow! What a waste!

Sadly, when my father finally died shortly after this conversation, I did not mourn. I realized that was because there was no loving, emotional bond. To this day, I envy people who suffer over the death of a parent because it means that there was so much love and attachment that the loss tears at their soul. I never had that with either parent.

My first memory from my childhood is one of my mother pulling me along the sidewalk on a rainy night while my father was in the car, rolling along the curb, begging her to get in. "The kid'll get sick!" he was yelling out the window. This pretty much represented their marriage. For reasons I never knew, they never appeared happy with each other. My father would never do nice things for her, while she was always annoyed with him.

My mother was a war bride from Italy. My father, a second lieutenant in the United States Army, met her in Gorizia after the American forces liberated northern Italy. My mother was an amazing beauty. When I was twenty-one and planning an anniversary gift for them, I asked my father what anniversary it was. Turns out that they were married in Italy, outdoors, under a beautiful tree when she was about five months pregnant with me. I actually liked hearing that I was a "love child," because it meant that there was at least one time when they had been happy with each other.

After the marriage, my mother, a nice Italian Catholic girl, came to America to meet my father's nice American Jewish family, and all hell broke loose. My father's mother went on a relentless attack against the "shiksa," the non-Jewish wife of a Jewish man. My grandmother tried to do everything she could to get rid of my mother and turned much of the family into rejecting her/us. When I was two and a half my mother, without my father, took me back to Italy for a few months, probably to get a break from this cruelty. My mother's parents were dead by this time, as was her older sister, who was killed by the Nazis on the first day she joined the underground resistance (I like to think that I channel her courage). Her brother survived, but she was not close to him.

We reunited back in the States, and over time it felt like there was always tension in our home, and I was always trying to smooth things over and make things better. My sister, eleven years my junior, and I really didn't have much bonding time because I left for college at seventeen (she was six) and never came home to live again. She and I handled the negativity in our home in different ways; she was more free-spirited, and I was more serious; this brought conflict between us and our lives, sadly, became very separate.

My parents finally divorced after my father had some "extracurricular activities," and he then married a nice woman with whom he lived until his death. My mother never re-married, and constantly expressed disdain for men, sex, and love. Neither one of them ever developed any close friend-ships at all. I felt responsible for her, while my sister gravitated toward my dad, who was feeling some guilt for the whole family mess and would indulge her.

I supported my mother financially, even though she had significant financial resources from her divorce and invest-ments, by hiring her as a receptionist in my counseling clinic. She had tried other jobs in clothing stores and such, but her poor people skills inevitably would cut her tenure short. At the clinic, she was abrupt with the counselors and on the phone, and she seemed to try to pit me against everyone else, I guess to have me all to herself. I put up with all of this out of a sense of obligation—I always took her on my vacations and bought her lovely gifts even when I had a modest income. She was never grateful and would always find something to criticize.

One day I gently asked if she would take a typing course, on my dime, because I needed help with the growing amount of paperwork I had as a therapist, writer, and college professor. She said, "No," picked up her stuff from the office, and refused to see or talk to me ever again. Once my mother scratched you off her list, you were off for life, even if you were her daughter. She had pathological pride.

So the years passed. She was not there for my son's birth, my home burning to the ground, my husband's near-fatal heart attack, nor the public attacks on me and my career by various special interest groups. After that, I frankly didn't care about her, either. There had never been any mother–daughter bond with me or with my sister.

One day the Beverly Hills police called me to let me know that my mother was dead and had been lying on the floor of her condo for about four months. Apparently she had no friends and none of her neighbors were close, so nobody even noticed! How sad.

The horrendous part of all of this is how the media, because I am a "celebrity," handled this event. I was accused by many of the network so-called news shows and radio talk show hosts of abandoning my mother, counter to what I espouse on my radio program. In fact, my mother alienated everyone in her life and *I* was being made to pay the price for it. One of the network morning news anchors asked some psychiatrist they grabbed at the last moment to comment on whether I should be allowed to give advice about family issues when I didn't have a relationship with my mother. My mother, I anguished, is causing me pain even after death!

Nonetheless, let me answer that question. That I did not have a loving, bonded family as a child disqualifies me from trying to help others create such in their homes? Huh? Of course not. If because I did not have a loving childhood I tried to undermine everyone else's attempts to have one, then I should be disqualified, no question. Everyone knows I'm a "family values" kinda girl, and because of my positions on marriage before children, hands-on parenting instead of institutionalized day care, divorce as a last recourse when there are minor children, and adoption instead of abortion, all hot-button issues, the messenger (me) was attacked in this vulgar, inhumane manner by media types who somehow see these values as threatening America. But life goes on. I know in my heart and mind what I've lived through and what I can live with, and I'm fine with that.

When my mother died, I didn't mourn. As with my father, there just wasn't any bonding. I did suffer, though. I was aware that both of my parents had an incredible impact on my life, as

I had difficulties being happy, building trusting friendships, being open, even relaxing. I didn't want to end up like either one of my parents, virtually alone and unloved.

But my resilience has paid off, and I'm doing the best I can with what I've got. I've built a life on the principle of helping others, and all in all I think it's turned out pretty well.